ANSWERS
Essential Music Theory
Levels 7-8

San Marco Publications

Mark Sarnecki

Elementary Music Theory © 2024 by San Marco Publications. All rights reserved.

All right reserved. No part of this book may be reproduced in any form or by electronic or mechanical means including Information storage and retrieval systems without permission in writing from the author.

ISNB: 9781896499499

Level 7-8 Answers

Page 2, No. 1

Page 4, No. 1

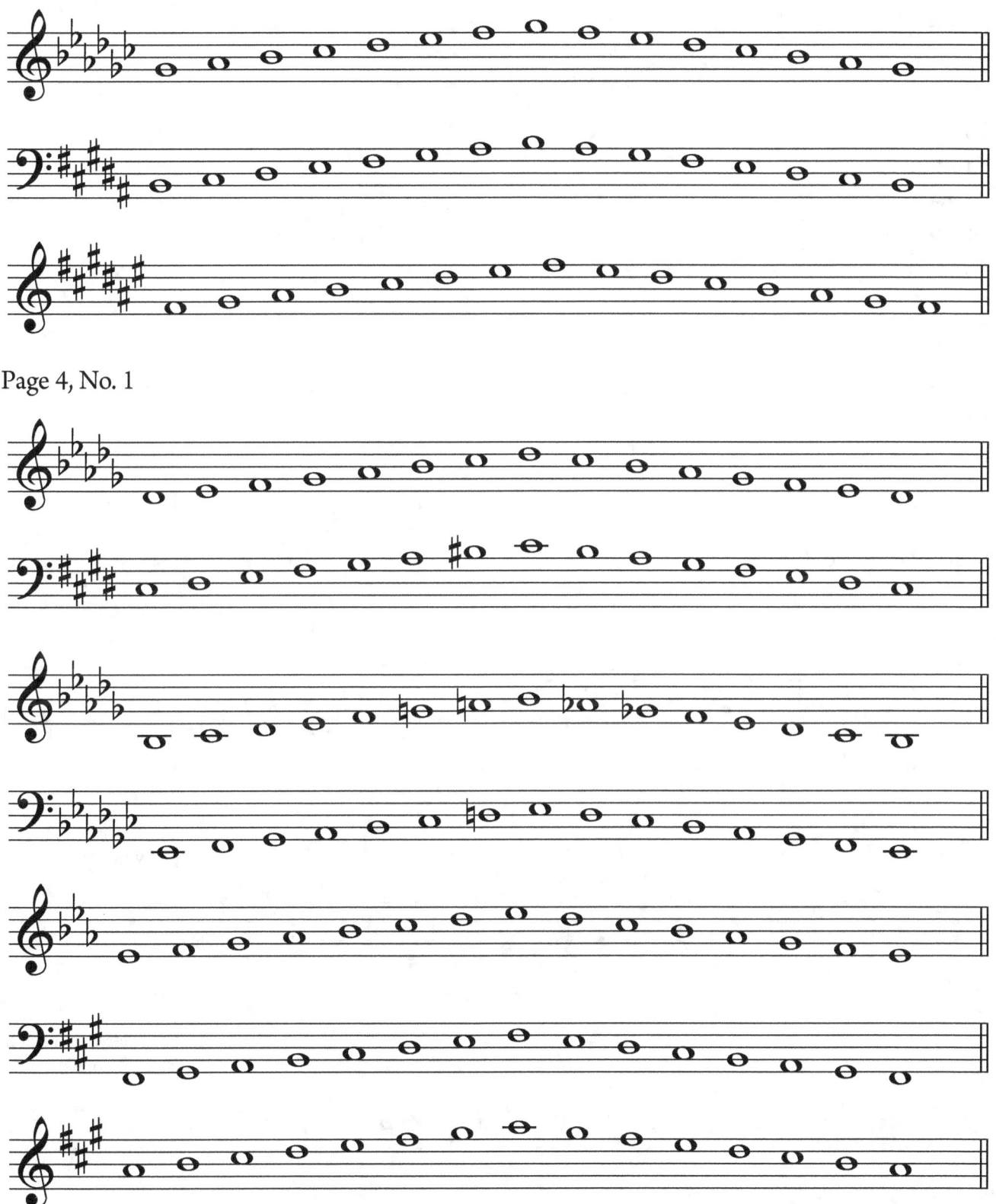

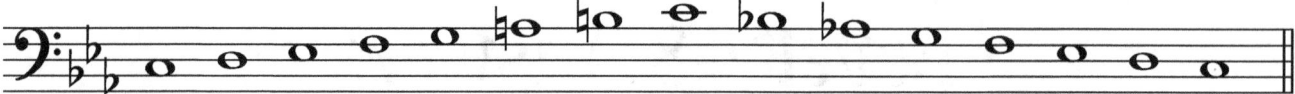

Page 7, No. 1

G major
B minor
C minor
E major
F minor
B♭ major
G♯ minor
A minor

Page 8, No. 2

C major
F major
D minor
G♯ minor

Page 10 - 11, No. 1

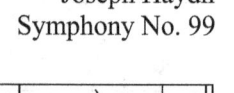

G minor

E♭ major

D minor

Frederic Chopin
Nocturne Op. 72. No. 1

E minor

Frederic Chopin
Sonata for Cello and Piano

D minor

Page 13 - 14, No. 1

Page 16, No. 1

Page 17, No. 2

Henry Purcell
Dido and Aeneas, Didos Lament

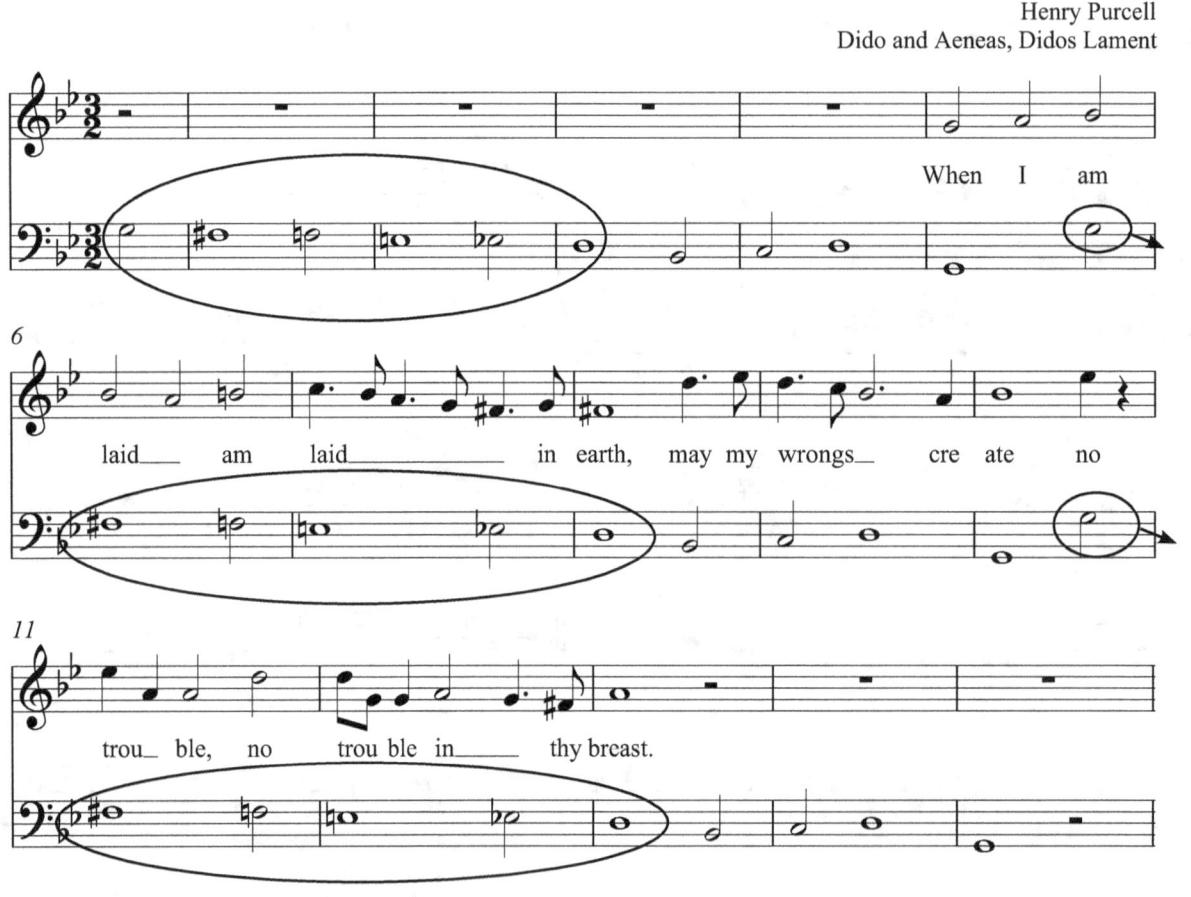

Page 19, No. 1

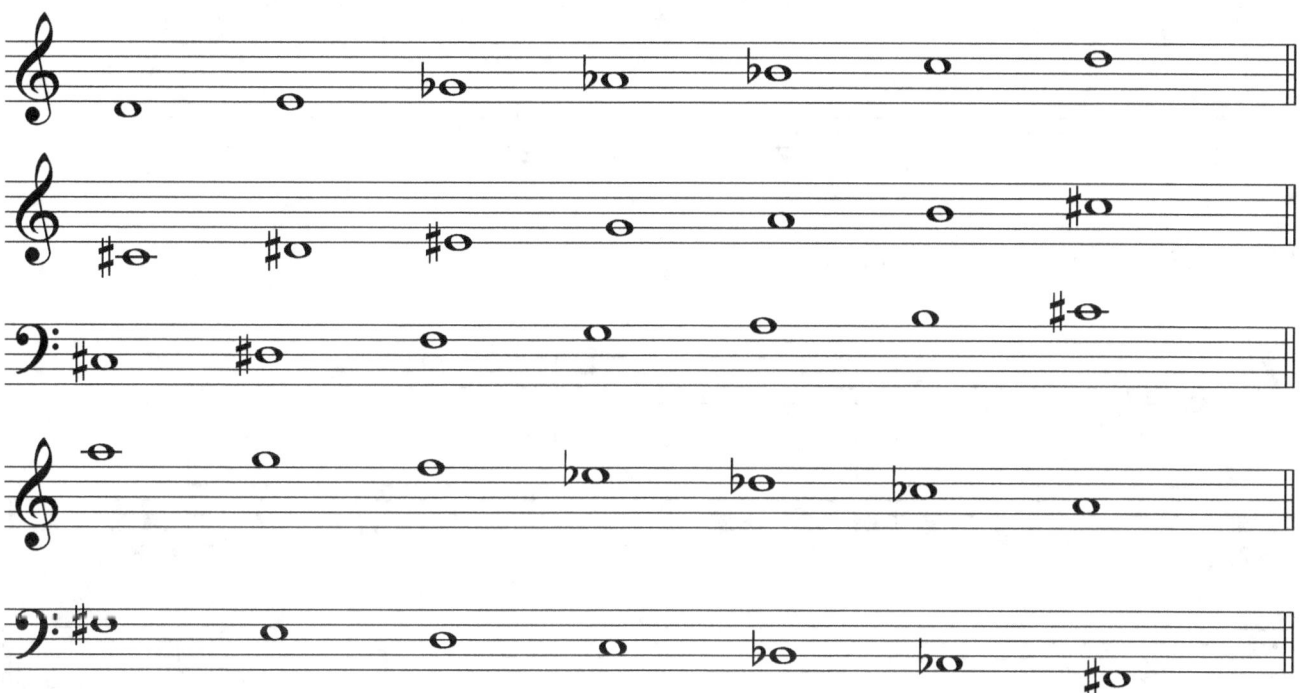

Page 19, No. 2 (other answers are possible)

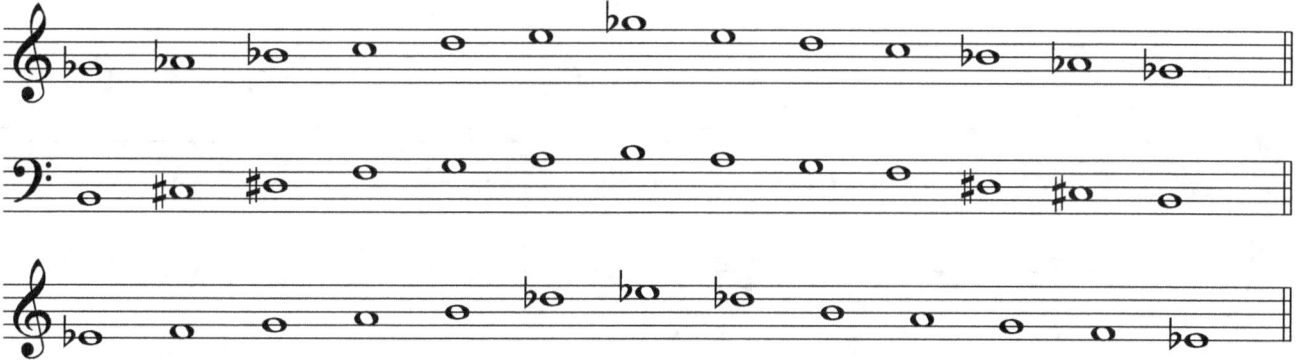

Page 21, No. 1 (other answers are possible)

Page 21, No. 2 (other answers are possible)

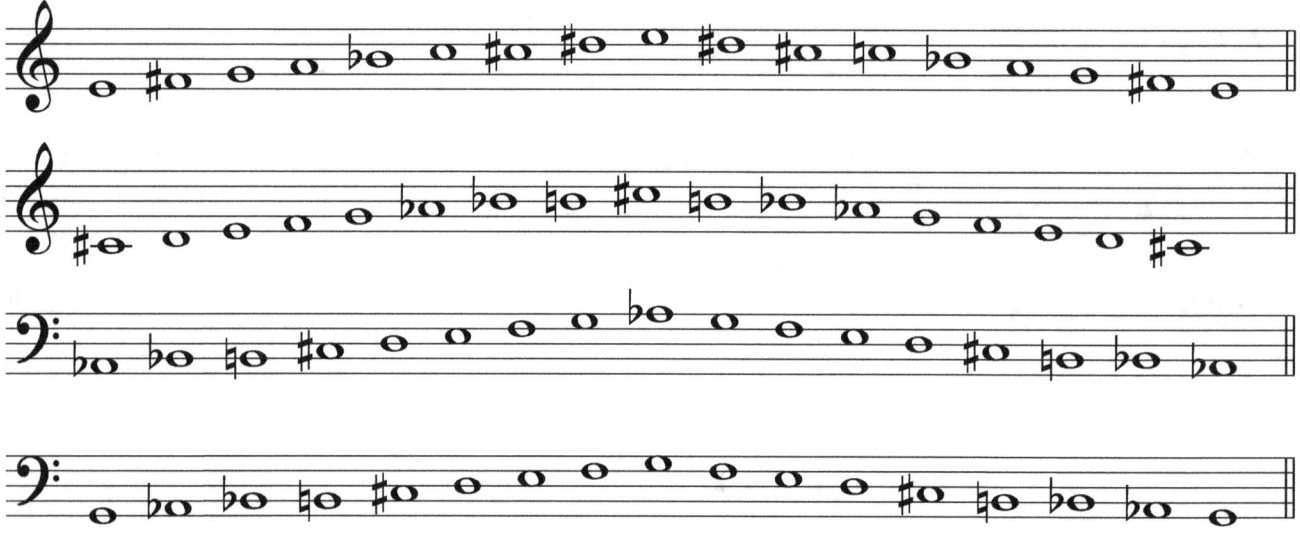

Page 22, No. 1

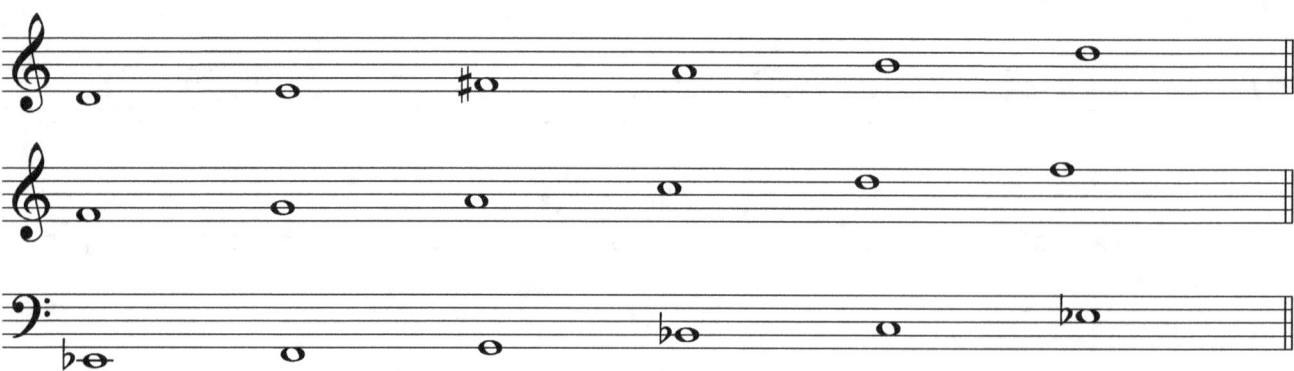

Page 23, No. 1

Page 24, No. 1

Page 25, No. 2

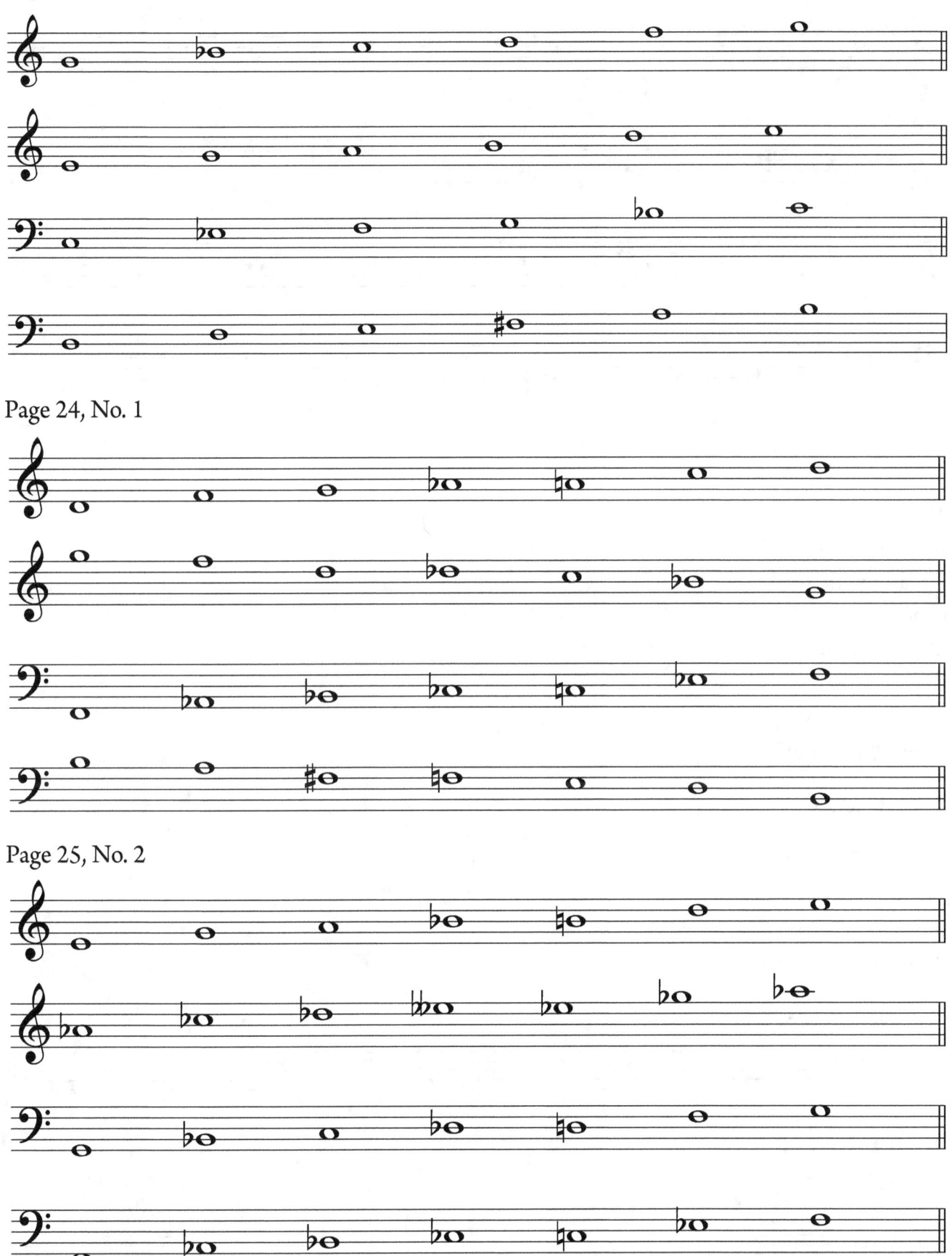

Page 25, No. 3

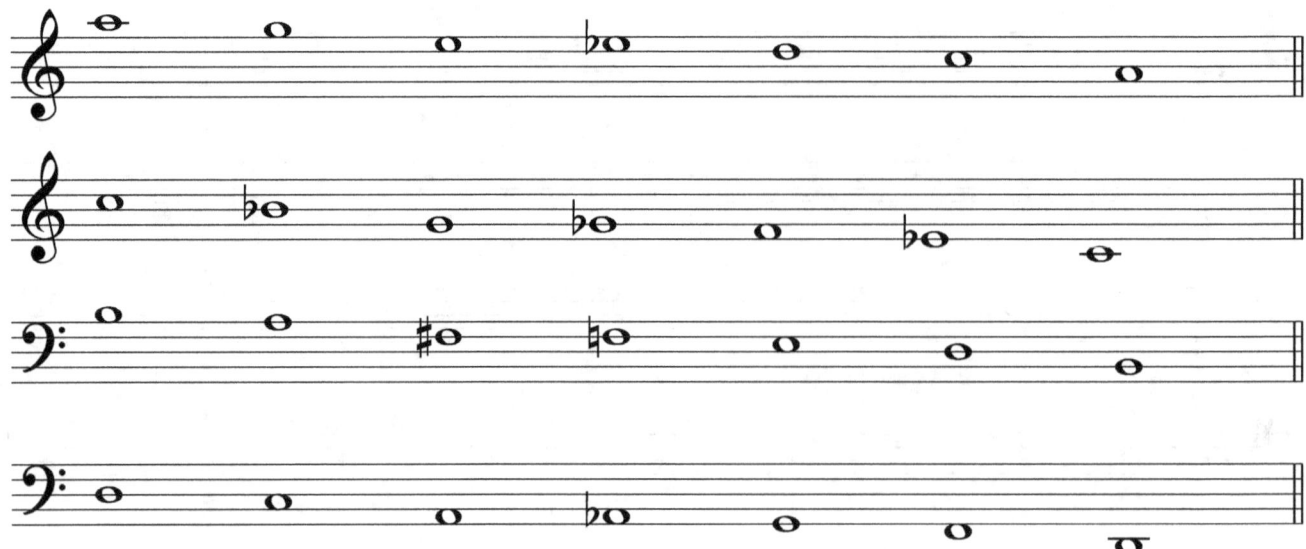

Page 26, No. 4

A♭ major
B melodic minor
E major pentatonic
C octatonic
D whole tone
F chromatic
D natural minor
A minor pentatonic

Page 29, No. 1

E A B F G C G F D

E B A E D D C G F

Page 29, No. 2

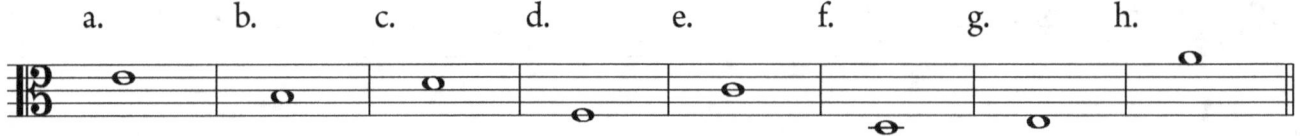

Page 29, No. 3

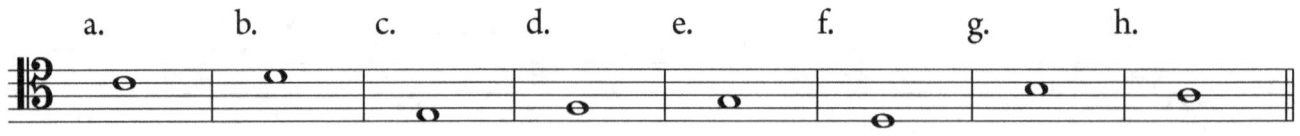

Page 30, No. 4

Wolfgang Amadeus Mozart
Cosi fan tutte

Page 30, No. 5

Gabriel Faure
Elegie, Op. 24

Page 31, No. 1

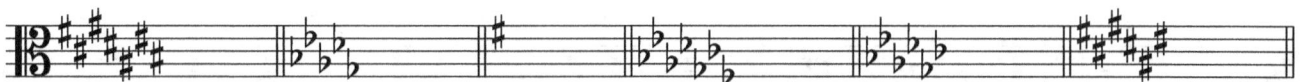

Page 31, No. 2

Page 36, No. 1

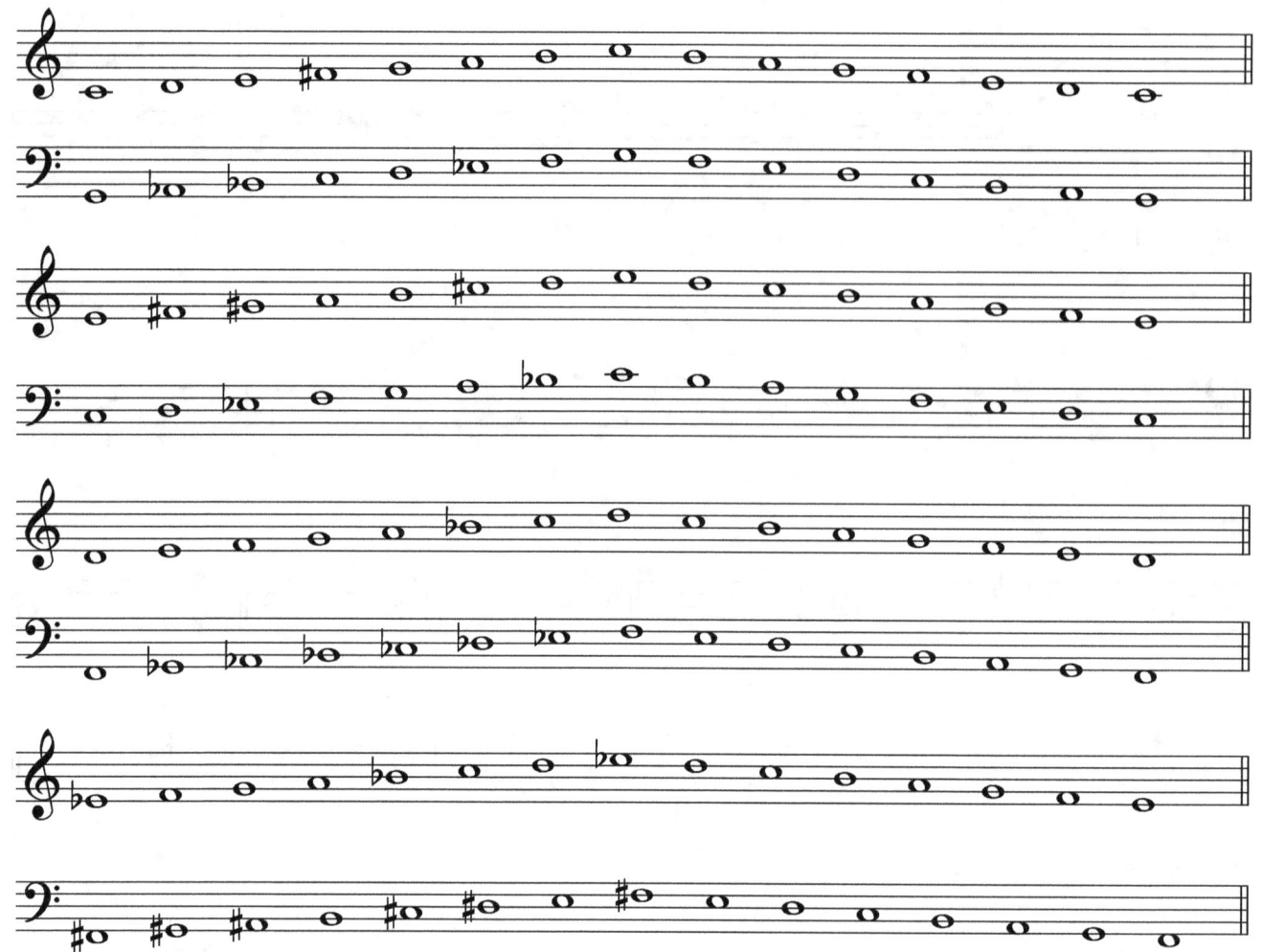

Page 37-38, No. 1

F dorian
G lydian
A locrian
E♭ mixolydian
G phrygian

B♭ mixolydian
D aeolian
F♯ dorian
B lydian

Page 40, No. 1

aug 5	min 6	per 5	maj 2	aug 3	aug 4
maj 3	per 8	dim 6	dim 5	dim 2	per 1

Page 41, No. 1

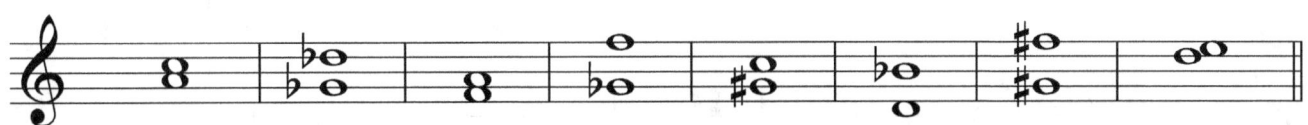

Page 43, No. 1

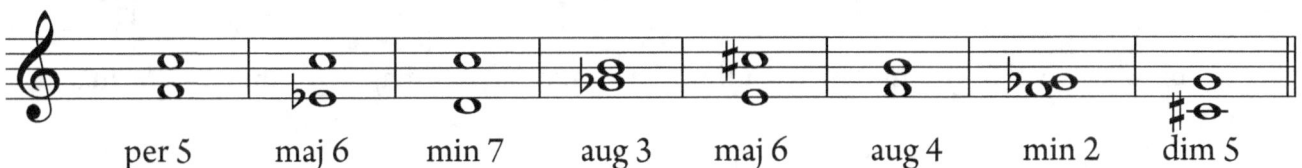

per 5   maj 6   min 7   aug 3   maj 6   aug 4   min 2   dim 5

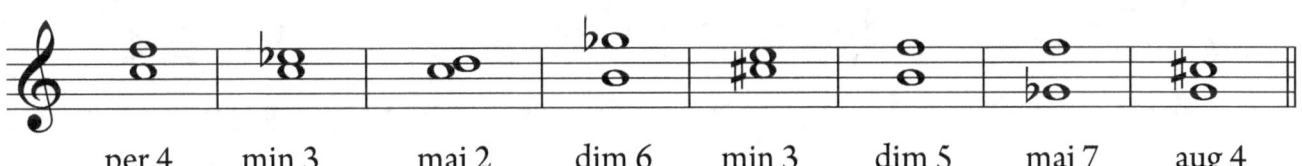

per 4   min 3   maj 2   dim 6   min 3   dim 5   maj 7   aug 4

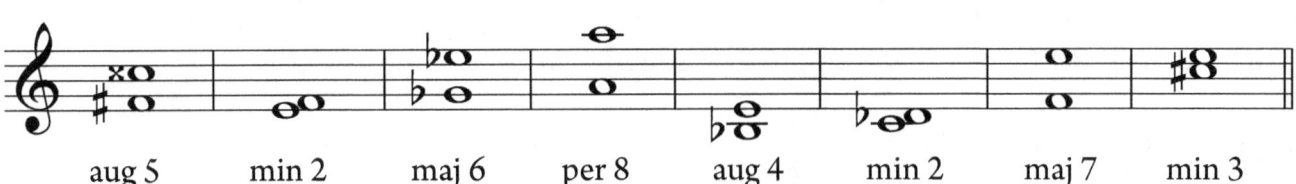

aug 5   min 2   maj 6   per 8   aug 4   min 2   maj 7   min 3

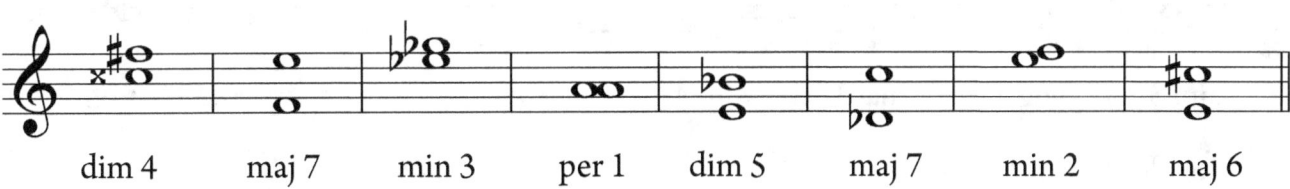

dim 4   maj 7   min 3   per 1   dim 5   maj 7   min 2   maj 6

Page 43, No. 2

dim 6   min 3   per 5   dim 4   aug 1   min 7   aug 8   min 6
maj 2   maj 7   maj 3   aug 8   dim 8   min 3   aug 4   min 7

Page 44, No. 3

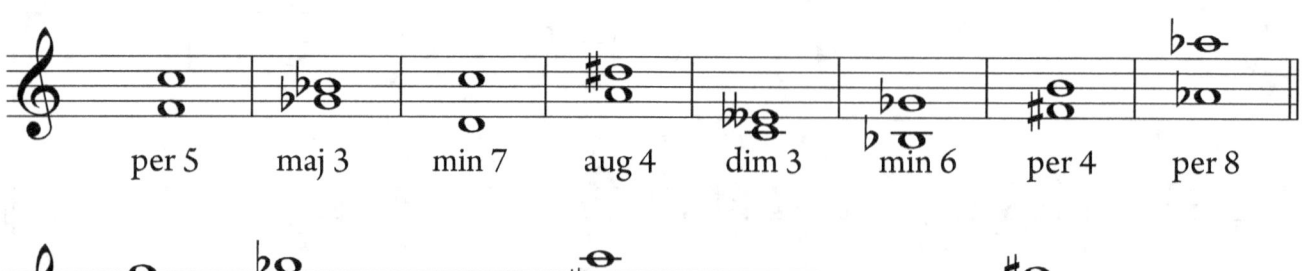

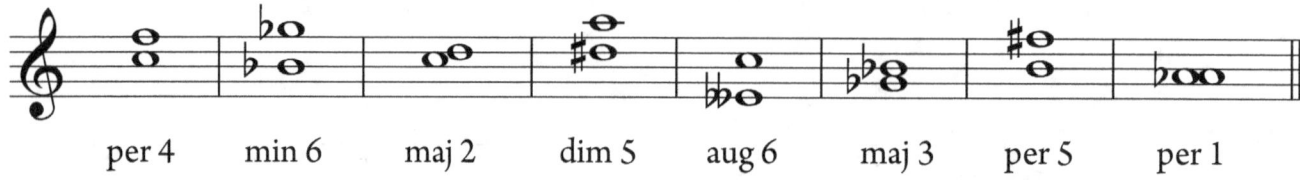

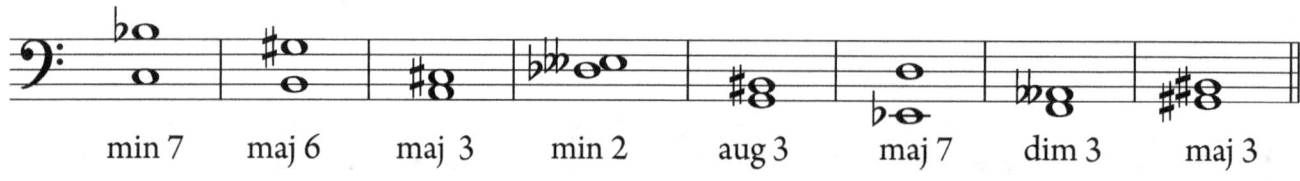

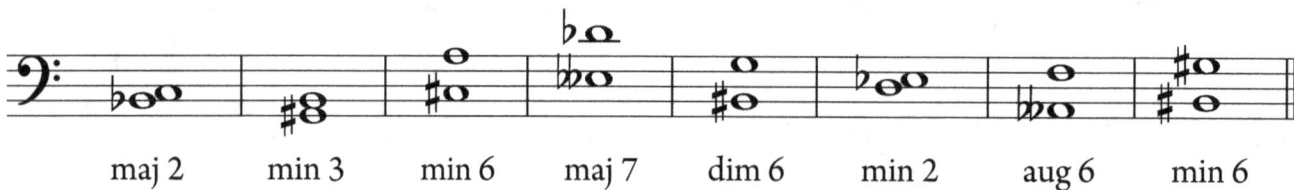

Page 44, No. 4

maj 2   dim 4   per 5   per 8   maj 3   min 2   min 3   maj 2

Page 45, No. 1

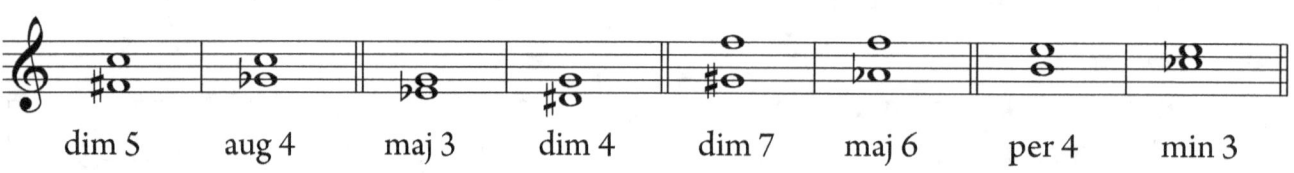

Page 45, No. 2

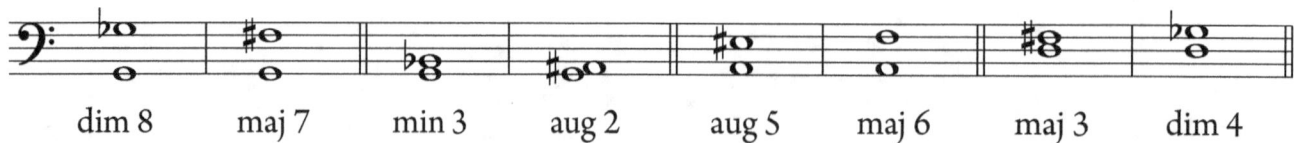

Page 51, No. 1

2, 3, 3, 3, 6, 7, 7, 7

Page 51, No. 2 and 3

Page 53, No. 1

Page 54, No. 2

12/8, 3/8, 9/4, 3/2, 6/16, 4/2, 6/8

Page 56, No. 1

Page 57 - 58, No. 1

Frédéric Chopin
Etude, Op. 10, No. 9

Frédéric Chopin
Waltz, Op. 69, No. 1

Giacomo Puccini
Madam Butterfly (One Fine Day)

Lili Boulanger
Nocturne

Page 60, No. 1

Page 62, No. 1

Page 63

Page 63, No. 2

Robert Schumann
Carnaval (Eusebius)

Franz Liszt
Hungarian Folksong No. 4

Johannes Brahms
Quintet Op. 111, II

Page 64, No. 1

Page 65, No. 1

Page 68, No. 1

Page 69, No. 2

Page 69, No. 3

Page 72, No. 1 (other answers are possible)

22

Page 74, No. 1

F	E♭m	Ddim	Caug	B♭	Am
G♭aug	F♯m	C	G♯	Adim	D♭aug
Em	Gm	Bdim	D	A♭	Baug

Page 74, No. 2

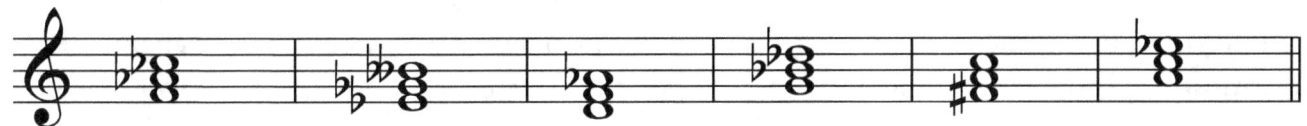

Page 74, No. 3

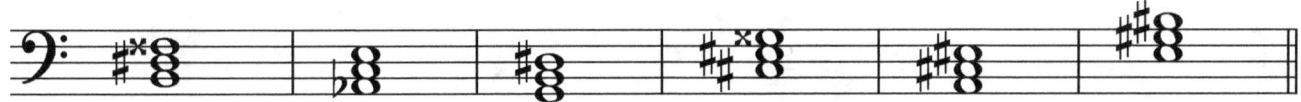

Page 74, No. 4

augmented   major   diminished   augmented   diminished   minor

Page 76, No. 1

F	C♯	A	E♭	D	B
major	minor	diminished	major	augmented	diminished
2nd inv	root pos	1st inv	2nd inv	root pos	1st inv
G	F♯	E♭	B	A	D♭
major	minor	minor	major	minor	major
root pos	2nd inv	2nd inv	root pos	1st inv	2nd inv
C	D	C	F♯	B♭	E
diminished	minor	major	major	major	minor
root pos	2nd inv	1st inv	root pos	2nd inv	root pos

Page 76, No. 2

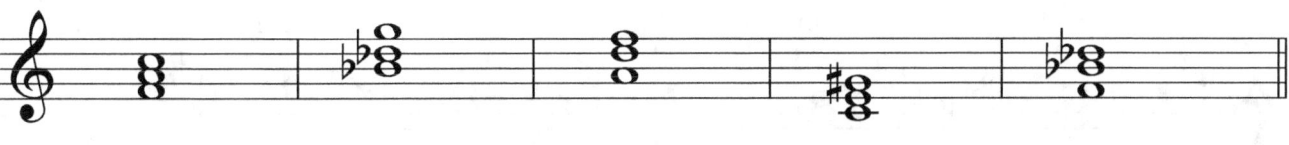

Page 77, No. 1

Symbol:	C/E	D♭aug	Am/C	G	Fdim/C	D
Root:	C	D♭	A	G	F	D
Quality:	major	augmented	minor	major	diminished	major
Position:	1st inv	root pos	1st inv	root pos	2nd inv	root pos

Symbol:	Bdim/F	Gm/D	A♭dim	F#/A#	Am	G#aug
Root:	B	G	A♭	F#	E	G#
Quality:	diminished	minor	diminished	major	minor	augmented
Position:	2nd inv	2nd inv	root pos	1st inv	root pos	root pos

Page 79, No. 1

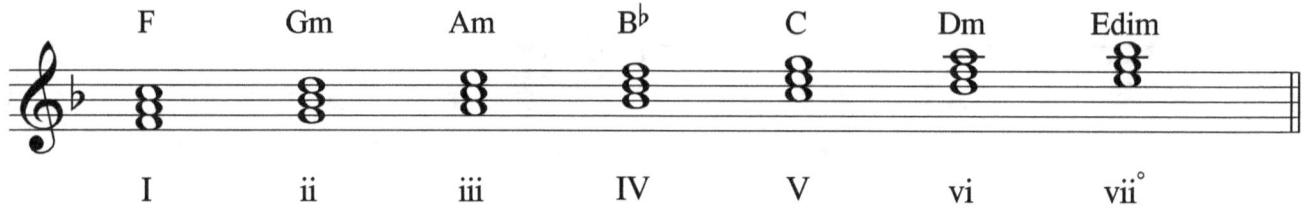

Page 79, No. 2

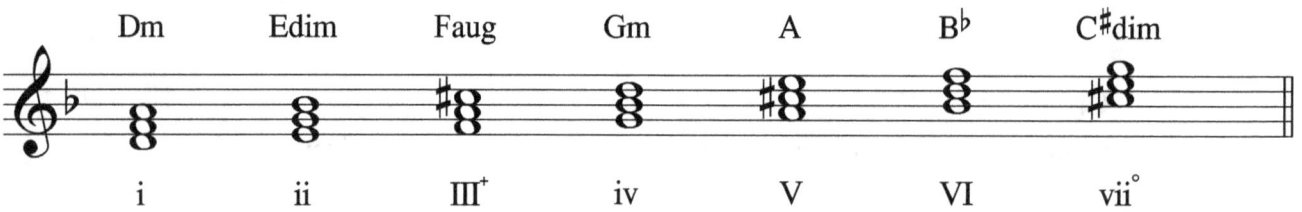

Page 80, No. 3

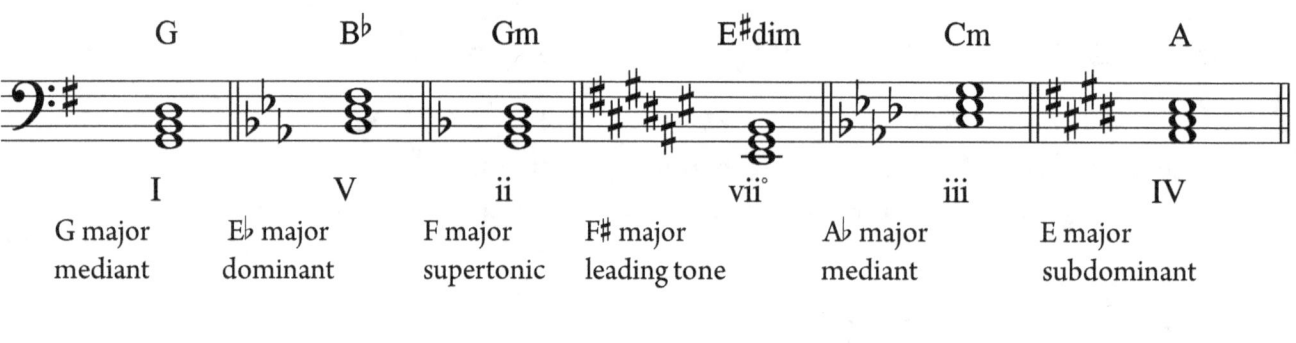

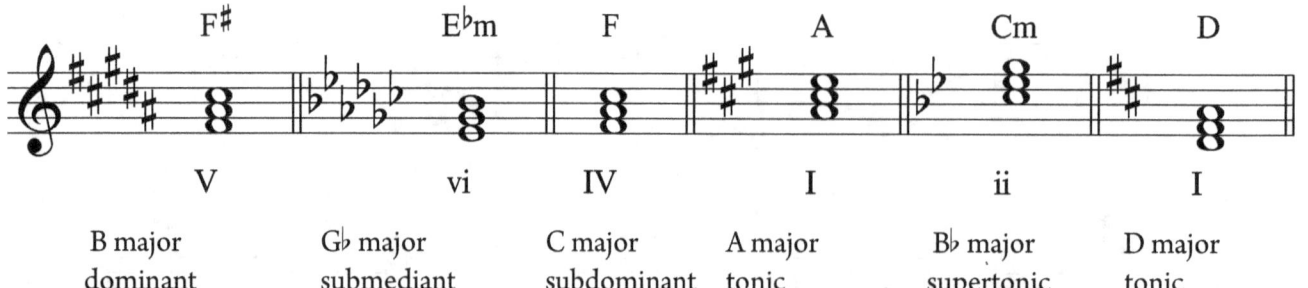

Page 80, No. 4

E minor leading tone | E♭ minor tonic | B minor supertonic | G minor mediant | F♯ minor mediant | B♭ ♮ supertonic

A minor dominant | D minor subdominant | C♯ minor submediant | C minor tonic | G♯ minor dominant | F minor leading tone

Page 81, No. 5

i. ii. iii. iv. v. vi.

Page 81, No. 6

i. ii. iii. iv. v. vi.

Page 81, No. 7

i. ii. iii. iv. v. vi.

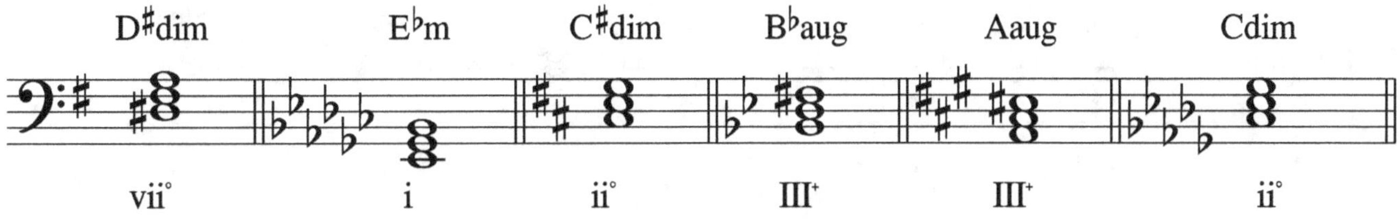

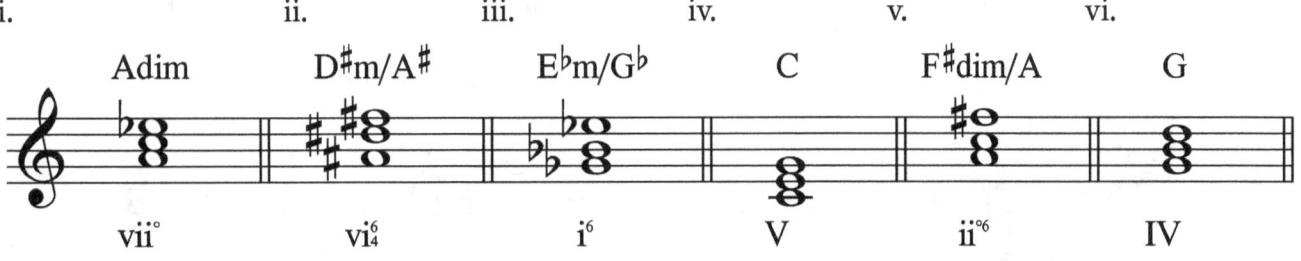

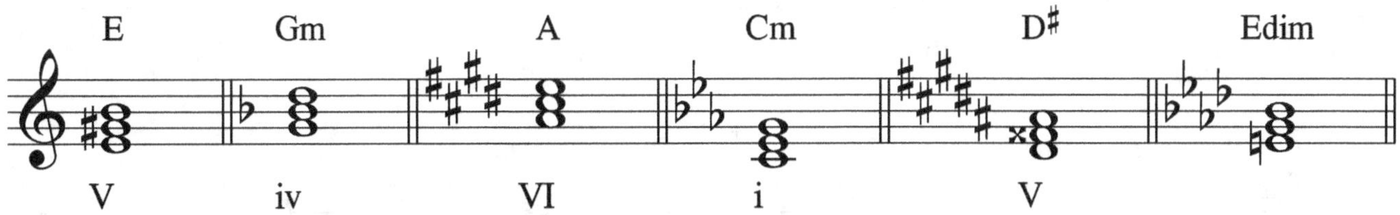

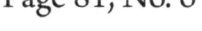

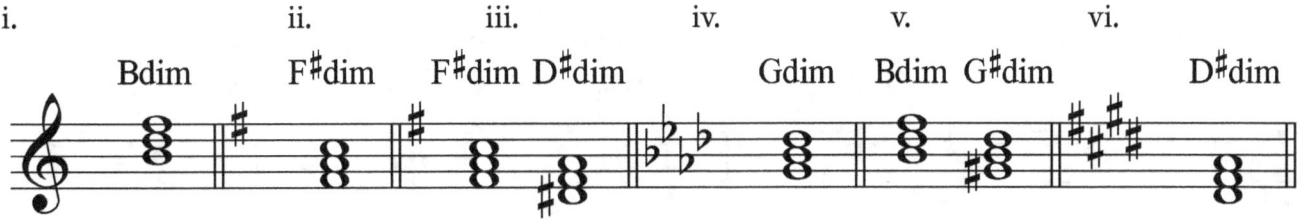

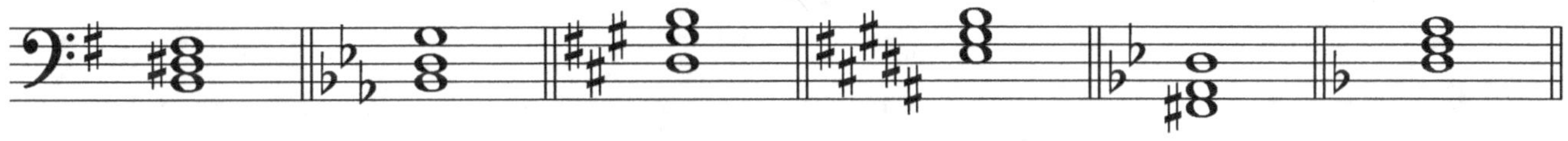

Page 84, No. 1

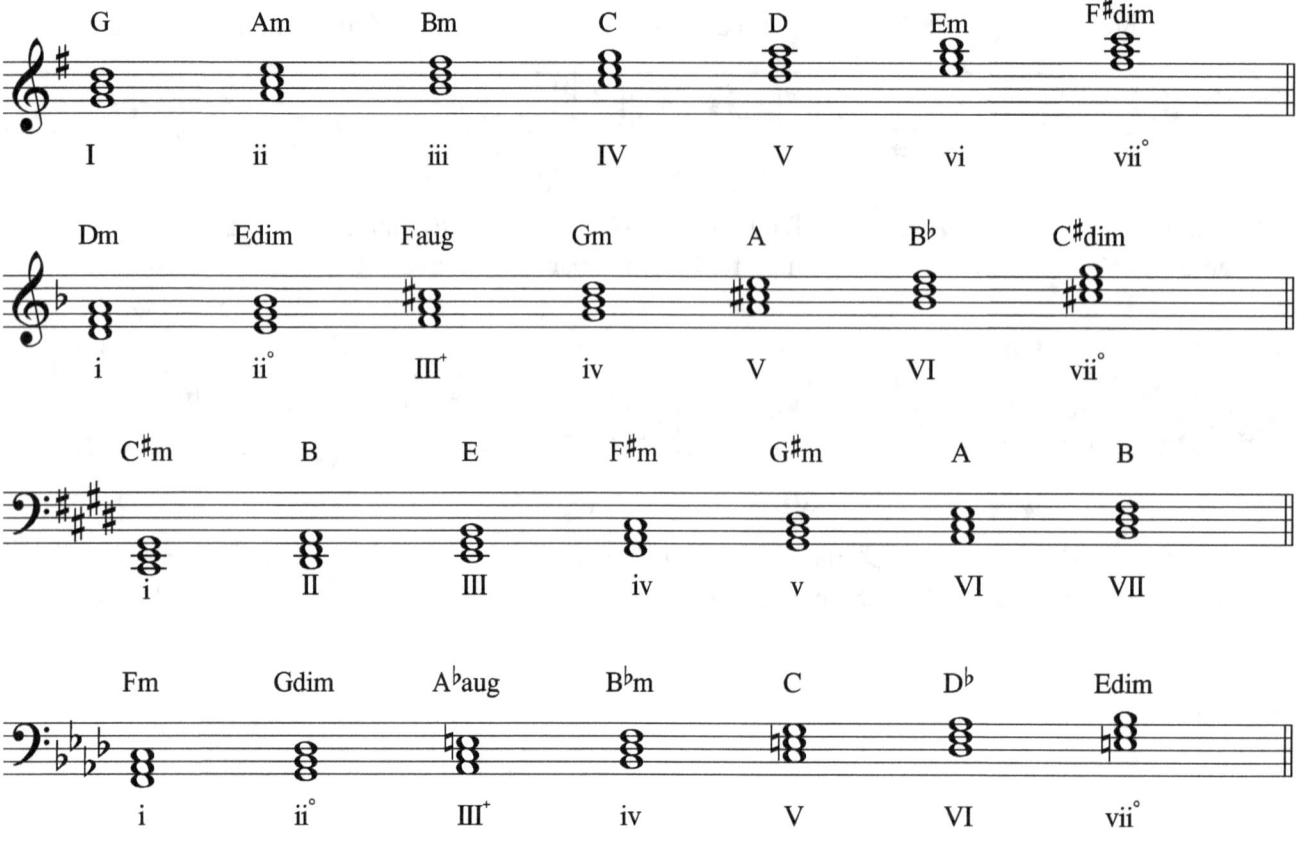

Page 84, No. 2

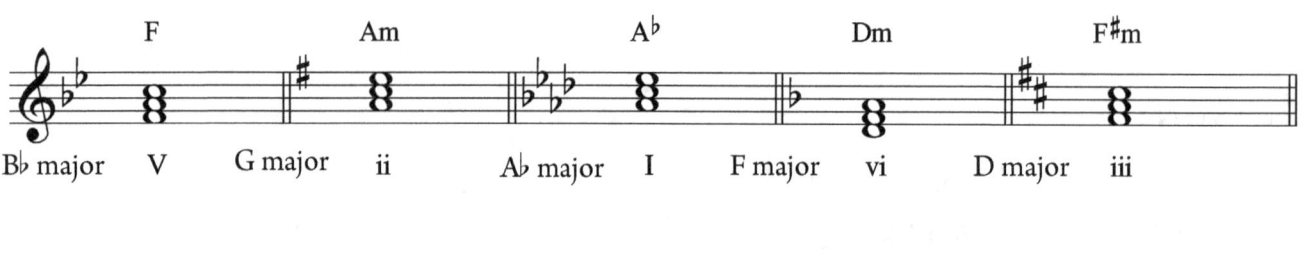

Page 85, No. 3

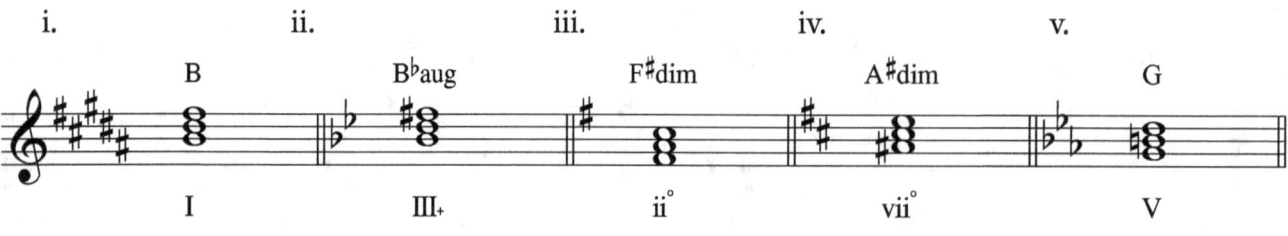

Page 85, No. 4

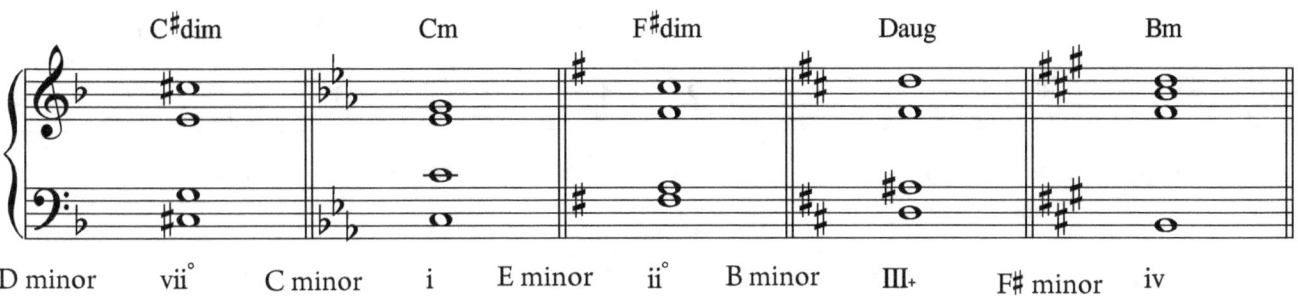

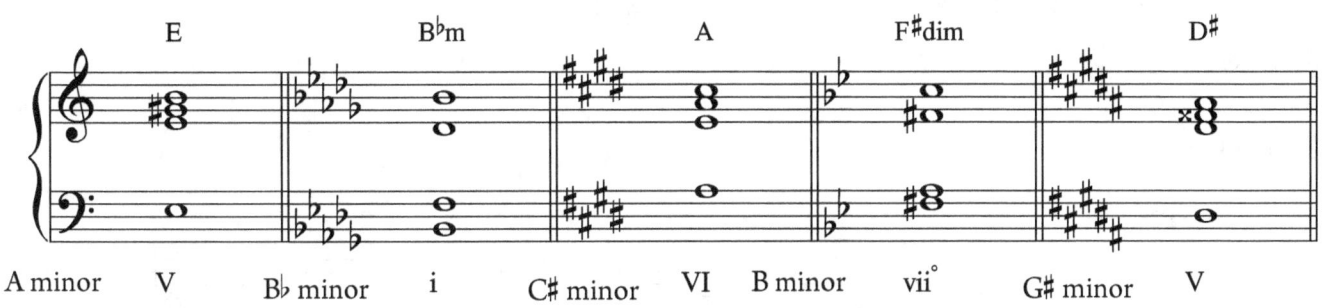

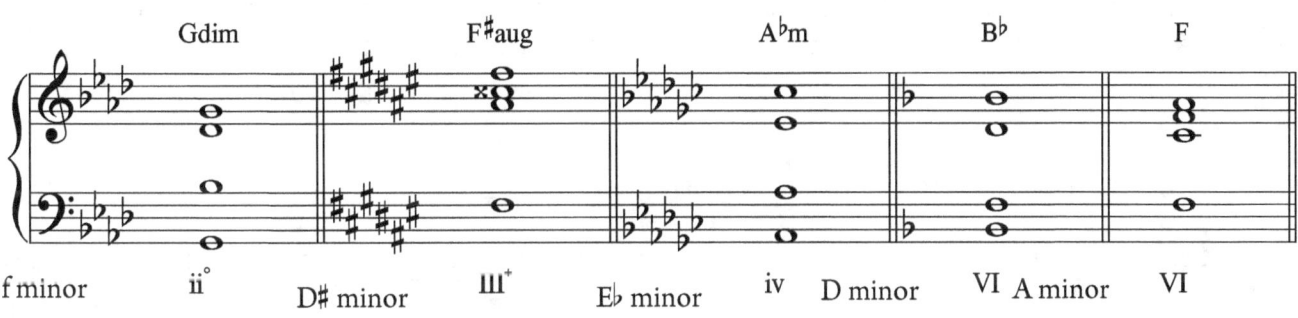

Page 87, No. 1

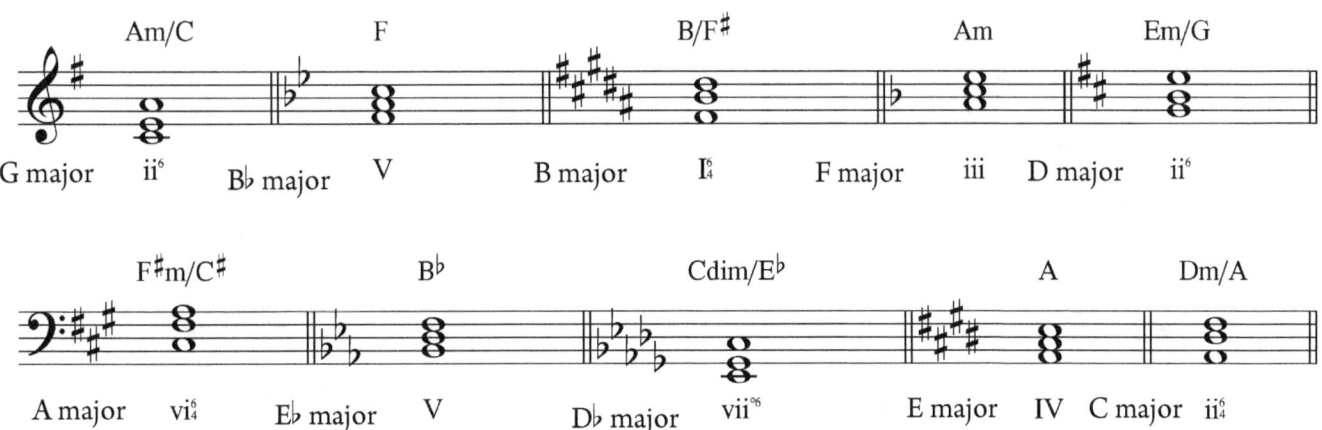

Page 87, No. 2

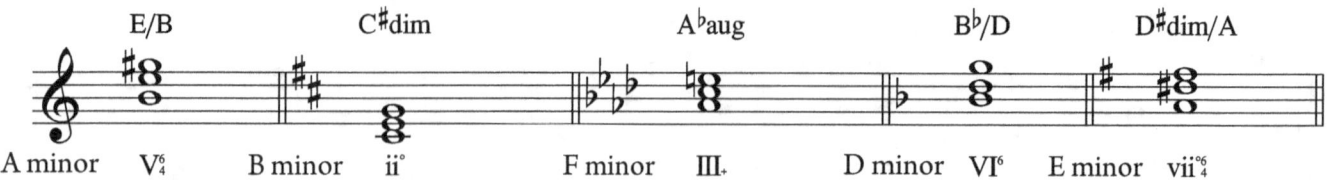

Page 88, No. 3

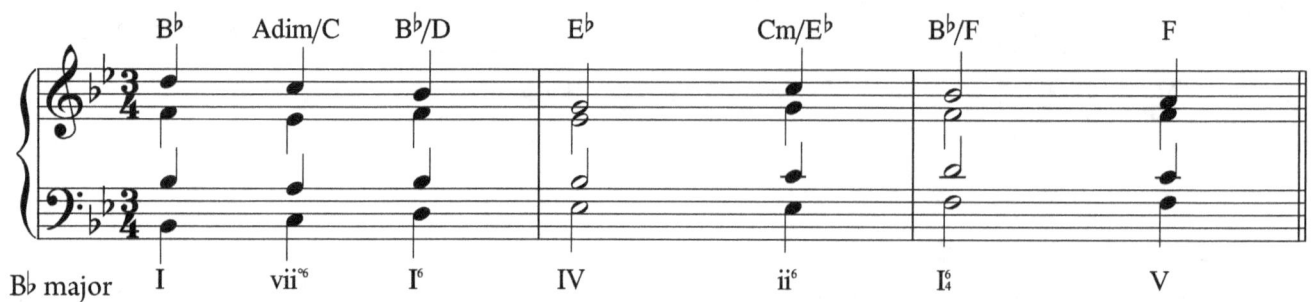

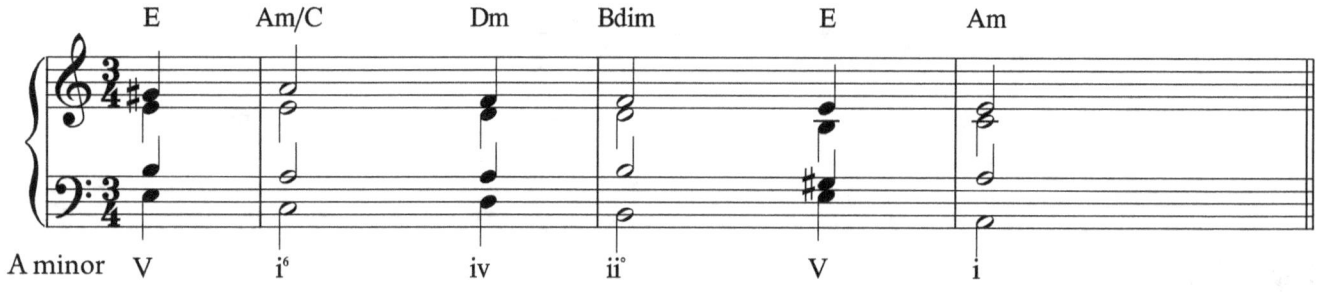

Page 90, No. 1

Key:	G minor	A major	B minor	F major
Root/quality:	D^7	E^7	F♯^{7}	C^7
Functional:	V^7	V^7	V^7	V^7

Key:	E major	F minor	B major	G major
Root/quality:	B^7	C^7	F♯^{7}	D^7
Functional:	V^7	V^7	V^7	V^7

Key:	E♭ major	D major	A minor	B♭ minor
Root/quality:	B♭^{7}	A^7	E^7	F^7
Functional:	V^7	V^7	V^7	V^7

Page 92, No. 1

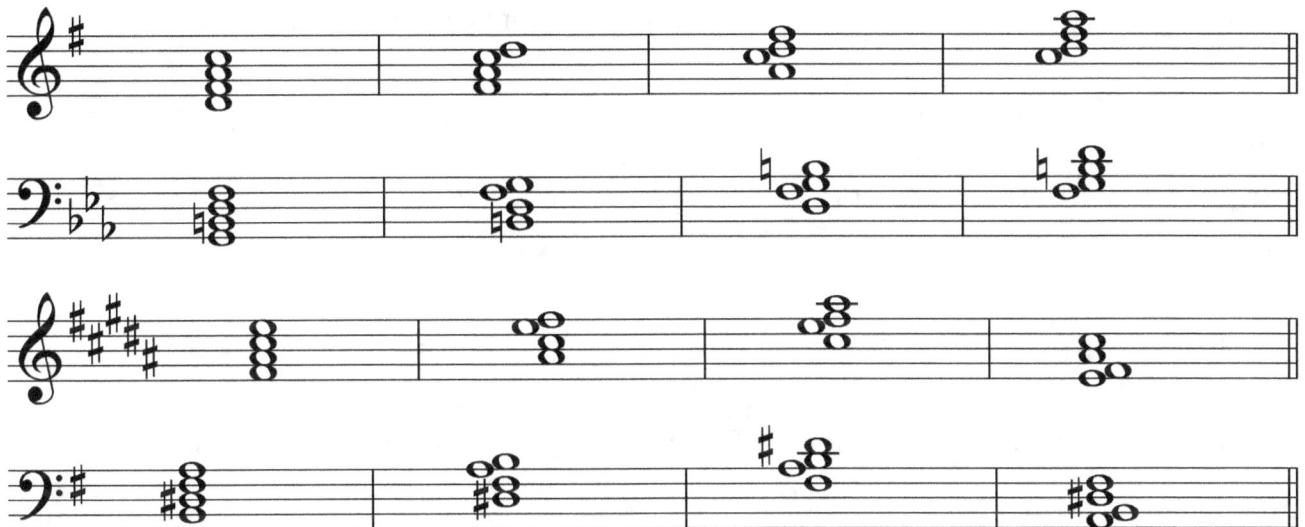

Page 92-93, No. 2

A♭	G	F	D	E	D♭
D♭ major	C major	B♭ major	G major	A major	G♭ major
D♭ minor	C minor	B♭ minor	G minor	A minor	G♭ minor
root pos	2nd inv	1st inv	3rd inv	1st inv	2nd inv

F♯	A♭	C	A	G♭	B♭
B major	D♭ major	F major	D major	C♭ major	E♭ major
B minor	D♭ minor	F minor	D minor	C♭ minor	E♭ minor
root pos	1st inv	3rd inv	1st inv	root pos	1st inv

Page 93, No. 3 (other answers are possible)

F major   G major   C major   E♭ major   E major   A major

F# major   B♭ major   E♭ major   A♭ major   G♭ major   D major

Page 93-94, No. 4

D	C	G	B	F#	E♭
G major	F major	C minor	E major	B minor	A♭ major
root pos	1st inv	1st inv	2nd inv	root pos	3rd inv

F#	B	D	F	A	A
B major	E minor	G minor	B♭ minor	D major	D minor
root pos	2nd inv	2nd inv	root pos	2nd inv	1st inv

Page 95, No. 1

D#dim⁷	F#dim⁷	E#dim⁷	C#dim	Bdim⁷	Fˣdim⁷
vii°⁷	vii°⁷	vii°⁷	vii°⁷	vii°⁷	vii°⁷
E minor	G minor	F# minor	D minor	C minor	G# minor

Page 95, No. 2

C minor   F minor   B minor   D minor   C# minor

vii°⁷   vii°⁷   vii°⁷   vii°⁷   vii°⁷

E♭ minor   F# minor   G minor   B♭ minor   A minor

vii°⁷   vii°⁷   vii°⁷   vii°⁷   vii°⁷

Page 95, No. 3

Page 96, No. 4

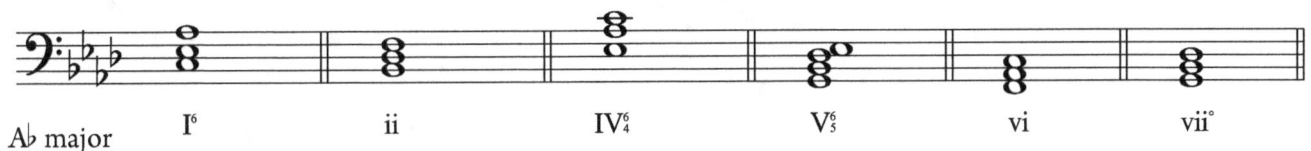

Page 98, No. 1

e.   d.   a.   h.   f.   b.   c.   g.

Page 102, No. 1

G major: D G   C minor: Cm G
                 V   I   i   V
                perfect authentic   half

D minor: A Dm   A♭ major: D♭ E♭
                 V i   IV V
                imperfect authentic   half

B minor: F# Bm   A major: E A
                 V   i   V I
                perfect authentic   perfect authentic

A minor: Am   E   D♭ major: A♭ D♭
                 i   V   V I
                half   perfect authentic

Page 106, No. 1 (other answers are possible)

Page 106, No. 2 (other answers are possible)

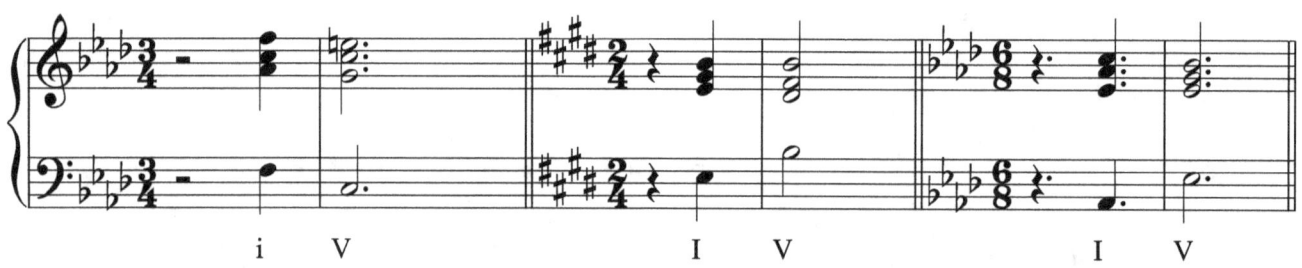

Page 106, No. 3 (other answers are possible)

Page 109, No. 1 (other answers are possible)

Page 110 (other answers are possible)

Page 111, No. 2 (other answers are possible)

Page 112-113, No. 1

	Gm Dm		F B♭
	iv i		V I
D minor:	plagal	B♭ major:	perfect authentic
	A E		Fm Cm
	IV I		iv i
E major:	plagal	C minor:	plagal
	Am E		E♭m B♭m
	i V		iv i
A minor:	half	B♭ minor:	plagal
	A D		Cm G
	V I		i V
D major:	imperfect authentic	C minor:	half
	E B		Bm C#
	IV I		iv V
B major:	plagal	F# minor:	half
	F G		D Gm
	IV V		V i
C major:	half	G minor:	perfect authentic

Page 115, No. 1 (other answers are possible)

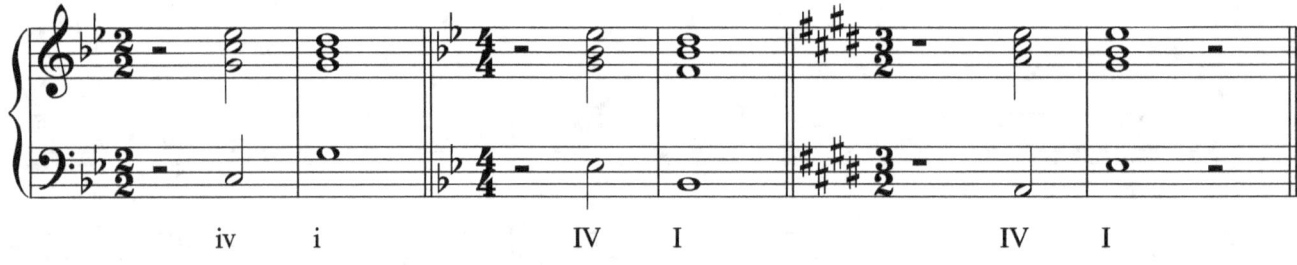

Page 119, No. 1 (other answers are possible)

Page 119, No. 2 (other answers are possible)

Page 121, No. 1 (other answers are possible)

Page 122, No. 2

Page 123, No. 3

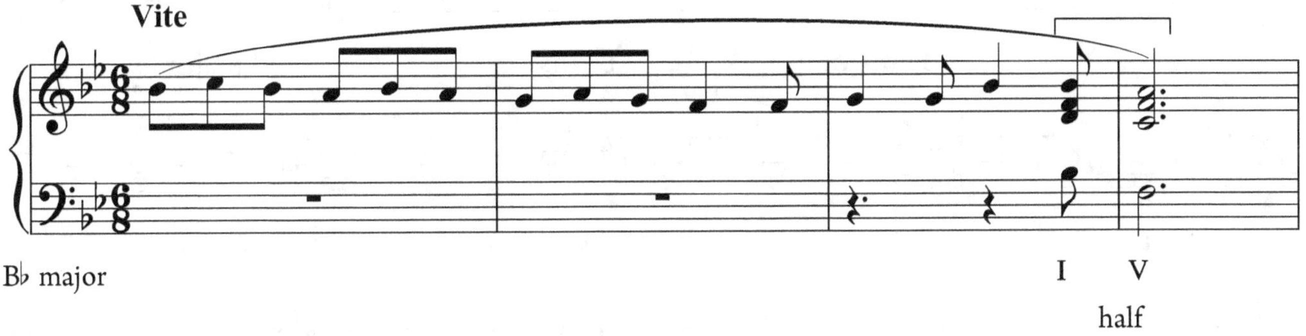
Vite
B♭ major
I
V
half

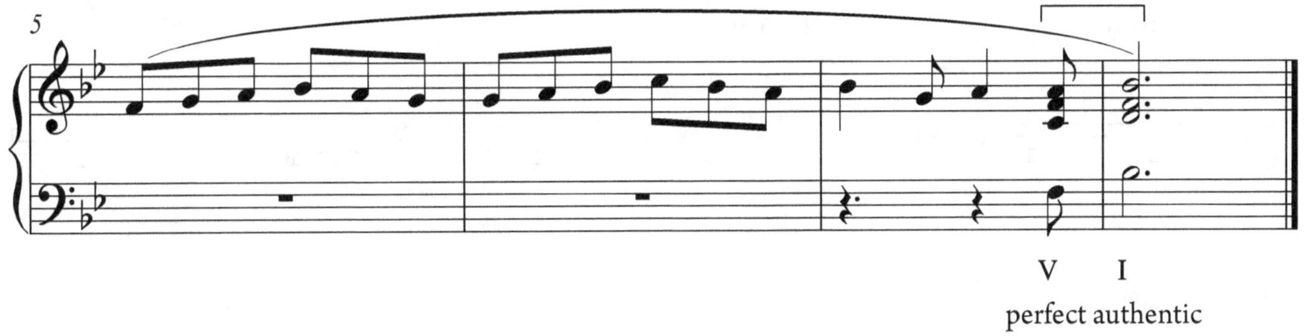
5
V
I
perfect authentic

Lentement
D minor
i
V
half

5
V
i
perfect authentic

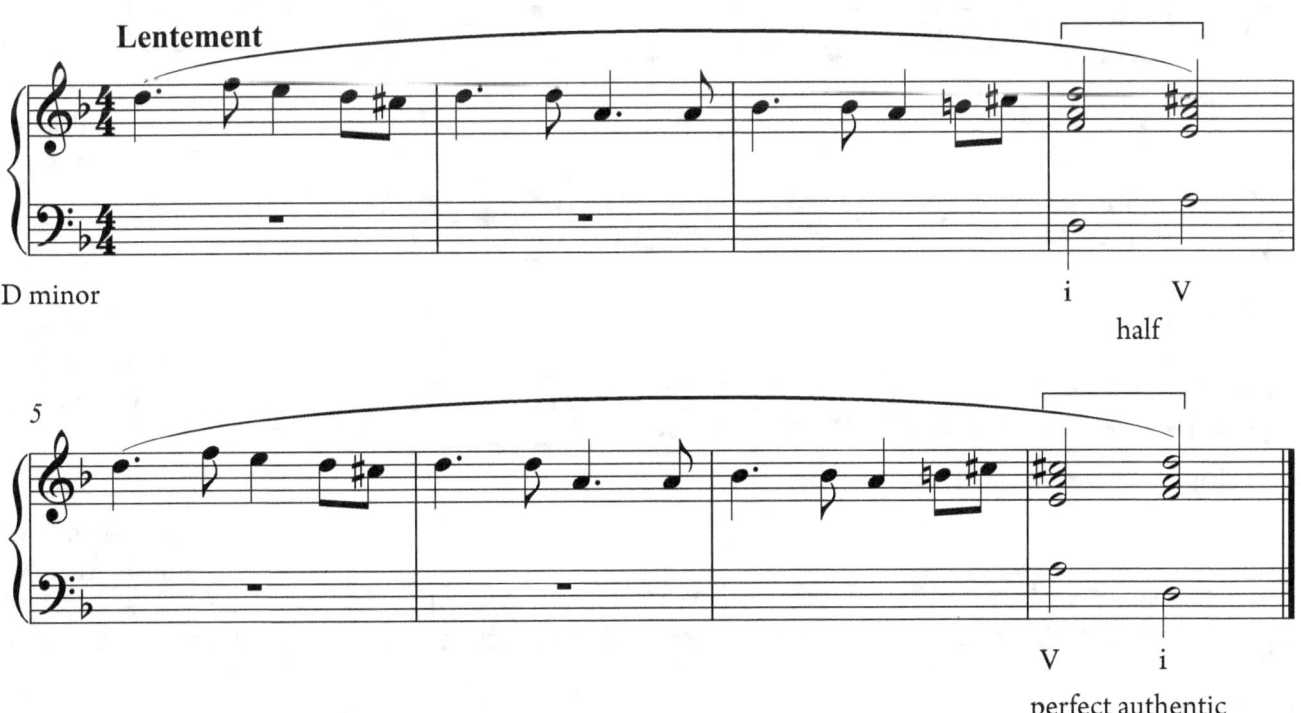

Page 125, No. 1

Page 126, No. 2

Page 128, No. 1

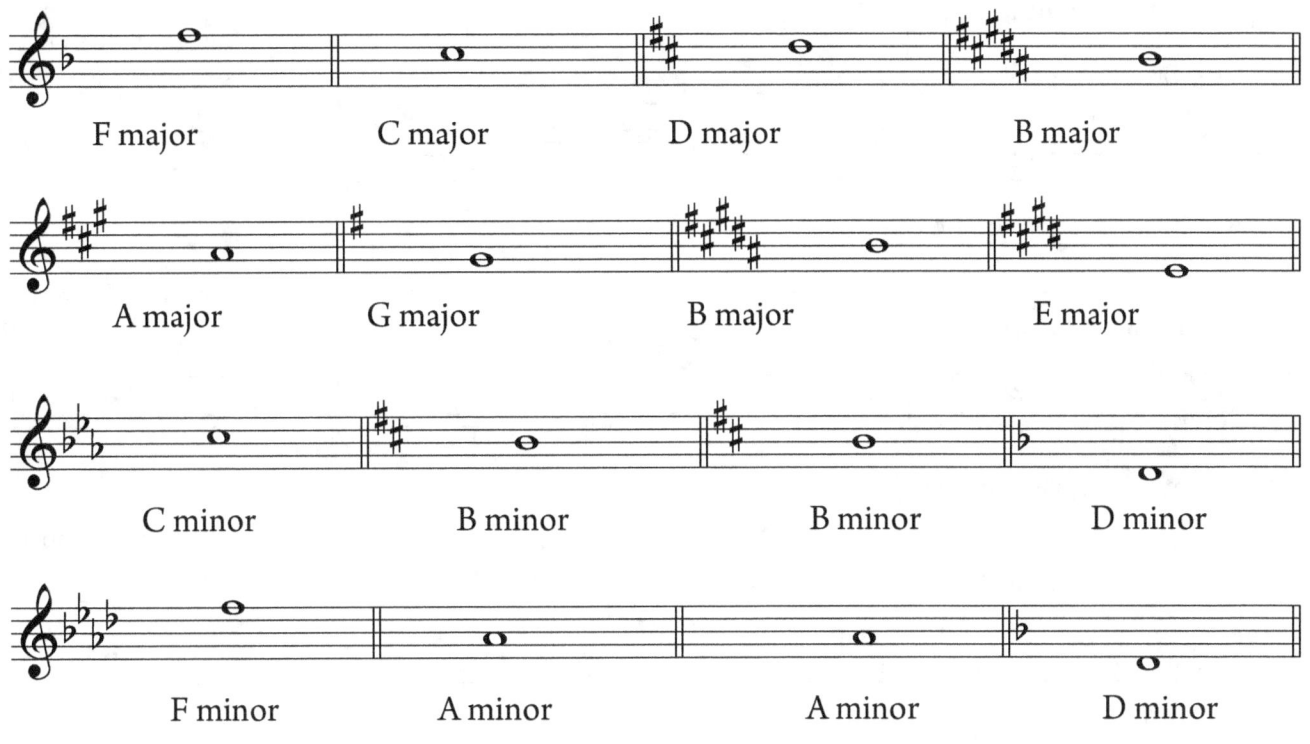

Page 129, No. 2

Original key: F major

Page 131, No. 1

Original key: G major

Andante maestoso

Ludwig van Beethoven
Symphony No. 9, IV

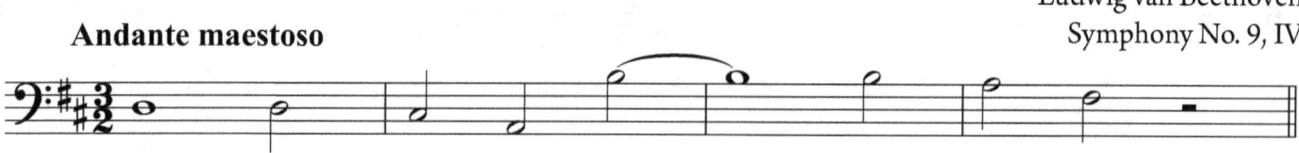

Interval of transposition: per 4

Andante maestoso

Ludwig van Beethoven
Symphony No. 9, IV

Interval of transposition: maj 3

Andante maestoso

Ludwig van Beethoven
Symphony No. 9, IV

Interval of transposition: min 6

Andante maestoso

Ludwig van Beethoven
Symphony No. 9, IV

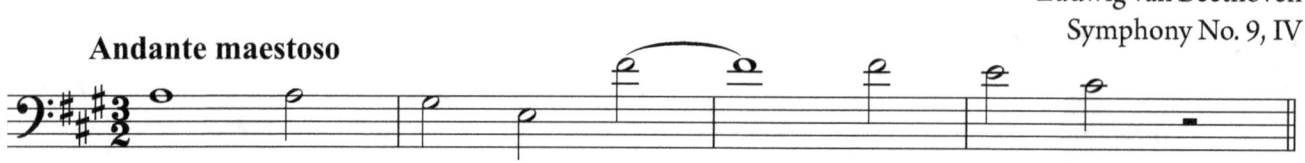

Interval of transposition: maj 2

Page 133, No. 1

C major

Allegro

Wolfgang Amadeus Mozart
Clarinet Concerto, K. 622

B♭ major

Page 134, No. 2

E♭ major

Allegro

Johann Nepomuk Hummel
Trumpet Concerto, III

F major

Page 134, No. 3

A minor

Allegretto

Wolfgang Amadeus Mozart
Symphony No. 40, Minuet

G minor

Page 135, No. 1

B♭ major

Allegro

Wolfgang Amadeus Mozart
Concerto for Horn, K.447, III

E♭ major

Page 136, No. 2

G minor

Allegro

Wolfgang Amadeus Mozart
Allegro, K.312

A minor

Allegro

Wolfgang Amadeus Mozart
Allegro, K.312

D minor

C♯ minor

Largo

Antono Vivaldi
The Four Seasons, Spring

G♯ minor

Largo

Antono Vivaldi
The Four Seasons, Spring

D♯ minor

Page 145, No. 1

Johann Sebastian Bach
Chorale no. 67: Freu' dich sehr, o meine Seele

Page 146, No. 2

Johann Sebastian Bach
Das walt' mein gott

Page 147, No. 3

Ludwig van Beethoven
String Quartet Op 18, No. 1

Allegro con brio

Page 148, No. 4

Franz Joseph Haydn
String Quartet Op 76, No. 3

Page 149, No. 5

Johann Sebastian Bach
O Haupt Voll und Wunden

Page 151, No. 1

E minor

F major

Page 153, No. 1

A minor

B♭ major

E major

F minor

B minor

Page 154, No. 2 (other answers are possible)

G major

B♭ major

D minor

E minor

Page 158, No. 1 (other answers are possible)

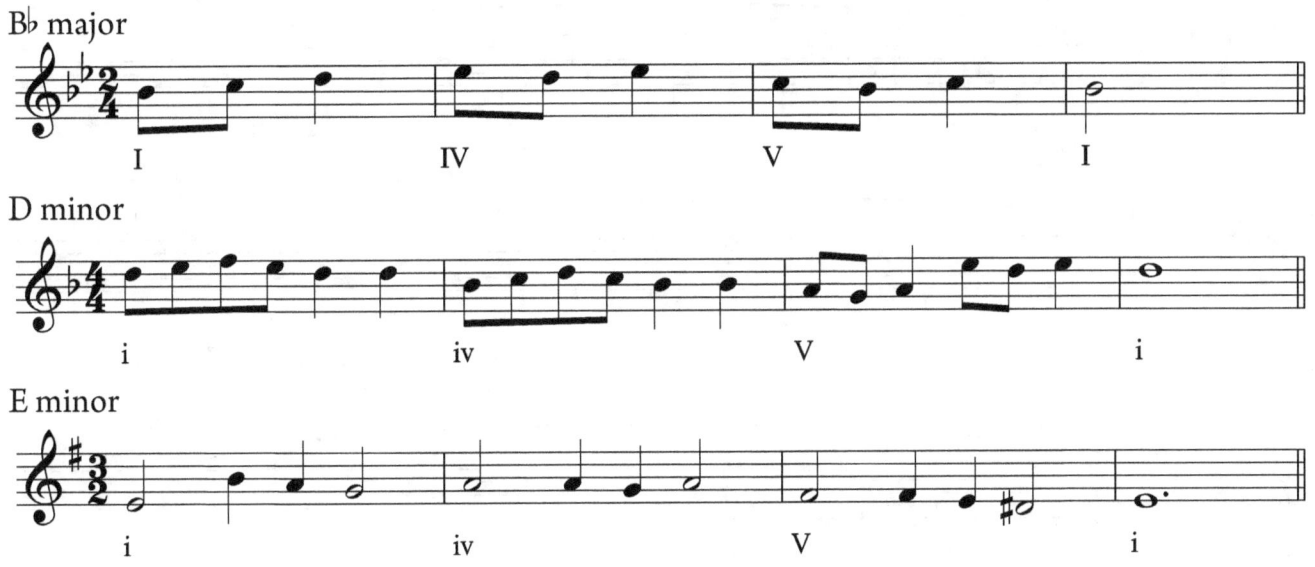

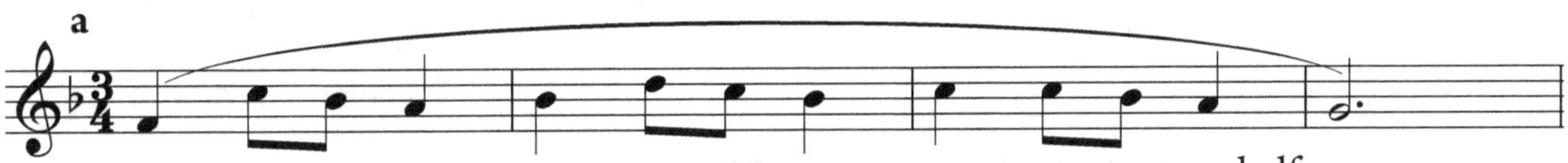

F major

half

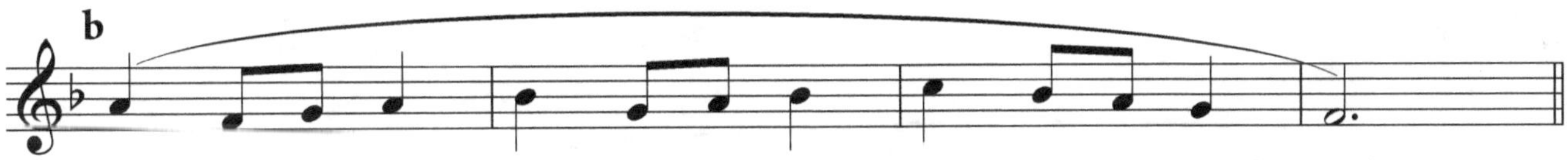

perfect authentic

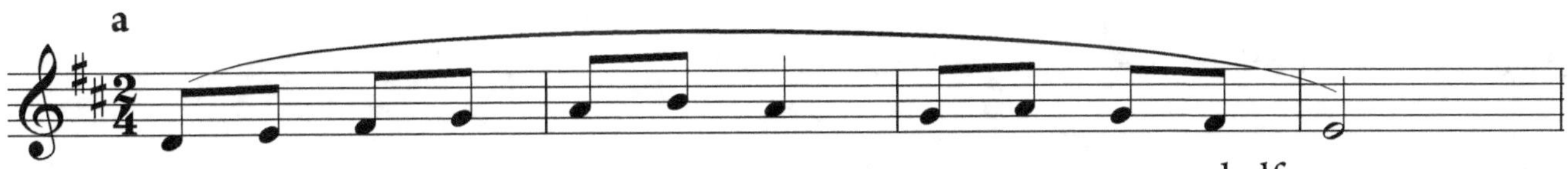

D major

half

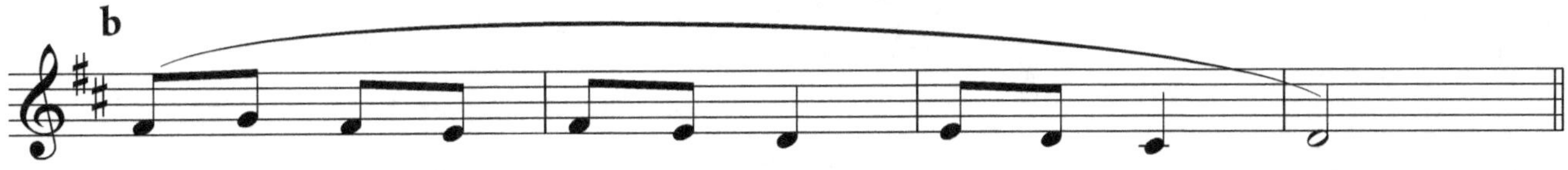

perfect authentic

a

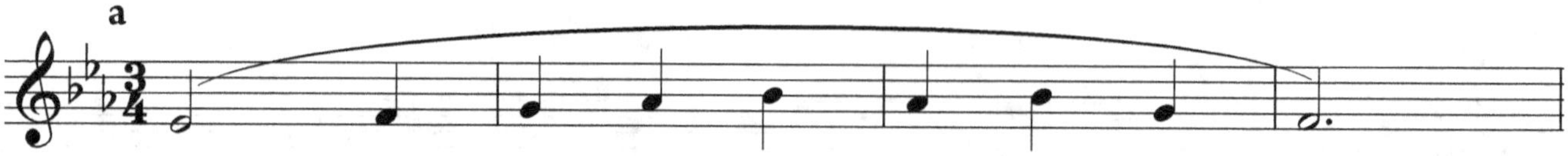

E♭ major half

b

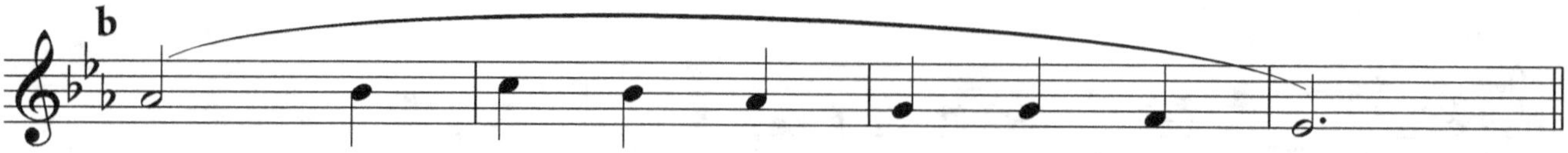

perfect authentic

a

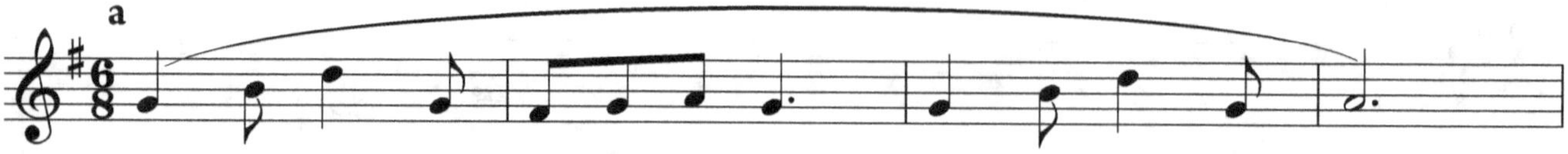

G major half

b

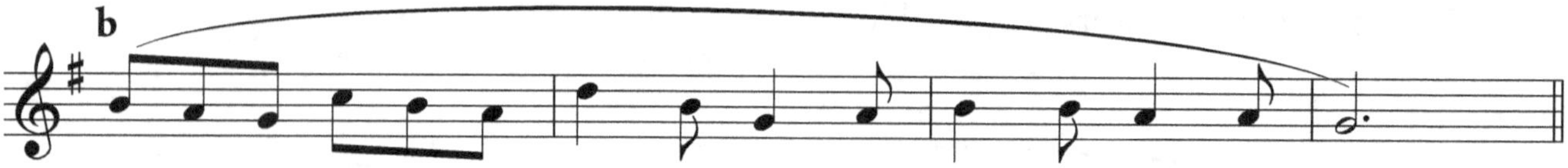

perfect authentic

a b

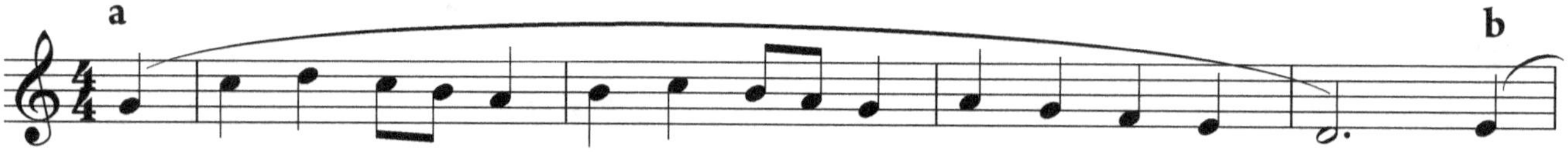

C major half

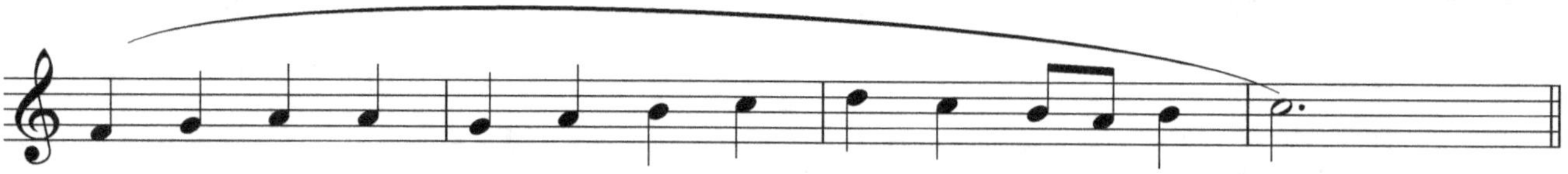

perfect authentic

Page 160, No. 1 (other answers are possible)

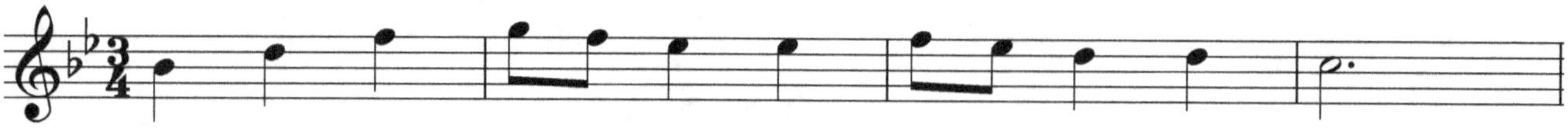

B♭ major I IV I V

5

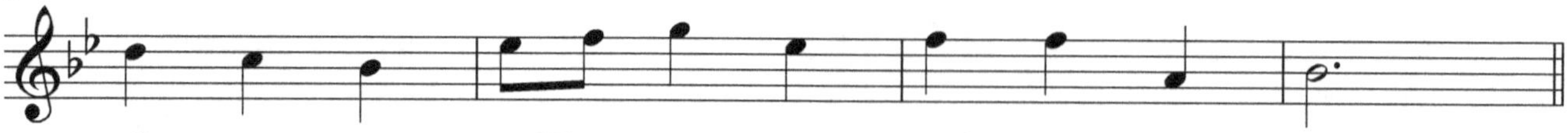

I IV V I

Page 161, No. 2 (other answers are possible)

B minor i   iv   i   V

i   iv   V   i

Page 177

a) When did the Romantic era occur? **1825 - 1900**

b) Music that has a literary or pictorial association is called **program music**

c) Name two Romantic period composers. **Franz Schubert, Frédéric Chopin, Franz Liszt, Robert Schumann, Johannes Brahms, Felix Mendelssohn, Edvard Grieg, Piotr Ilyich Tchaikovsky, Guisseppe Verdi, Georges Bizet**

d) Where was Felix Mendelssohn born? **Germany**

e) Whose music did Mendelssohn help revive? **J.S. Bach's**

f). What genre is Overture to a Midsummer Nights Dream? **Concert overture**

g) What author wrote the play that this work is based upon? **Shakespeare**

h) What is the form of Overture to a Midsummer Nights Dream? **Sonata form**

i) Name the three main sections in this form. **Exposition, Development, Recapitulation**

Page 177

a) F, b) F, c) T, d) T, e) F, f) F, g) T, h) T

Page 178

Petrushka
Composer: Igor Stravinsky Genre: Ballet

Koko
Composer: Duke Ellington Genre: 12 bar blues

Dripsody
Composer: Hugh LeCaine Genre: electronic music

Etude Op. 10, No. 12 'Revolutionary'
Composer: Frédéric Chopin   Genre: solo piano piece

Overture to a Midsummer Nights Dream
Composer: Felix Mendelssohn   Genre: concert overture

Page 190, No. 1

E minor:	V iv V i		B minor:	iv V i
F major:	I IV V		A minor:	iv V i
D minor:	iv V i		E major:	I IV V I
G♭ major:	I IV V I		G♯ minor:	i V i

Page 190, No. 2

1. tonic   2. dominant   3. subdominant   4. tonic

Page 191, No. 1

A major: I V V
C minor: i V iv

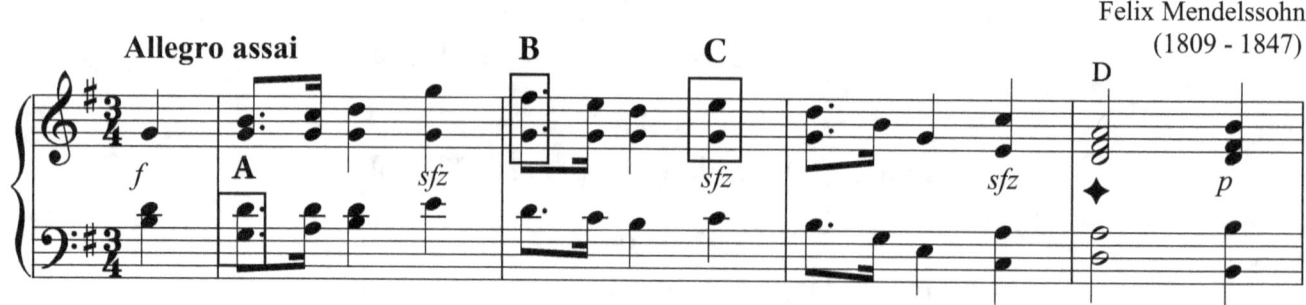

1. Felix Mendelssohn
2. Overture to a Midsummer Nights dream
3. Romantic era
4. 8
5. G major
8. per 5, maj 7, maj 6, aug 4
9. very fast
10. sforzando, sudden strong accent
11. perfect authentic
12. Because the piece begins with an incomplete measure or anacrusis.

1. Romantic era
2. A♭ major
3. 3/4
4. D♭ major
5. subdominant chord
6. E♭ major
7. dominant chord
8. C: neighbor tones   D: passing tones
9. fairly fast, a little slower than allegro
10. fortepiano, loud than suddenly soft
11. stable

Page 194

George Frideric Handel
(1685 - 1759)

1. George Frideric Handel

2. Messiah

3. Baroque era

4. D minor

5. 3/2

6. simple triple time

7. tonic chord

8. dominant chord

9. subdominant chord

10. 4

11. D: min 3rd   E: min 3rd   F: min 3rd

12. 4

13. 7

Page 195

Johannes Brahms
(1833-1897)
Weigenlied Op. 49 No. 4

1. E♭ major

2. 3/4

3. homophonic texture

4. Romantic era

5. Frédéric Chopin, Felix Mendelssohn, Robert Schumann, Pyotr Tchaikovsky, Franz Liszt

7. min 3

8. maj 3

9. dim 5

Page 196, No. 1

Sensucht nach dem Fruhling

Wolfgang Amadeus Mozart
(1756- 1791)

a. Name the key of this piece. **F major**
b. Write the time signature directly on the score. **6/8**
c. In what musical period was this piece composed? **Classical**
d. Mark the phrases directly on the score.
e. Is this an example of a: ☑ parallel period   ☐ contrasting period
f. Mark the form on the score using the letters **a**, **a¹**, or **b**.
g. State the implied harmony using functional and root/quality chord symbols.
h. Circle and identify any non-chord tones.

55

Sonatina

III

Allegro
Matthew Camidge
(1758- 1844)

a. Name the key of this piece. **D major**
b. Write the time signature directly on the score. **6/8**
c. In what musical period was this piece composed? **Classical**
d. Mark the phrases directly on the score.
e. Is this an example of a: ☑parallel period ☐contrasting period
f. Mark the form on the score using the letters **a, a¹,** or **b**.
g. State the implied harmony using functional and root/quality chord symbols.
h. Circle and identify any non-chord tones.
i. Write the name of the cadences at the end of each phrase in the place provided on the score.

Page 199, No. 1

contrary	oblique	parallel	similar
oblique	parallel	contrary	parallel
similar	oblique	contrary	oblique

Page 200, No. 1

Page 200, No. 2

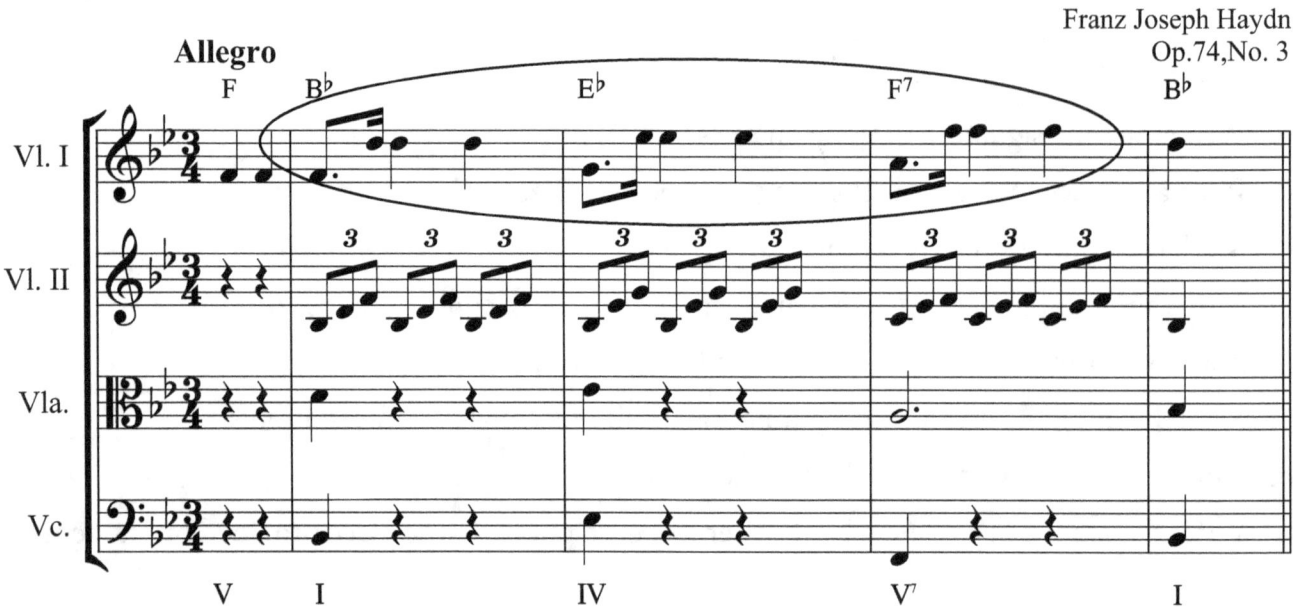

a. Name the key of this phrase. **B♭ major**
b. Write the time signature directly on the score. **3/4**
c. In what musical period was this piece composed? **Classical**
d. What open score is this written for? **String quartet**
e. State the implied harmony using functional and root/quality chord symbols on the score.
f. Find and circle a melodic sequence.
g. Name the cadence at the end of this phrase. **Imperfect authentic**

Passepied

George Frideric Handel
(1685-1759)

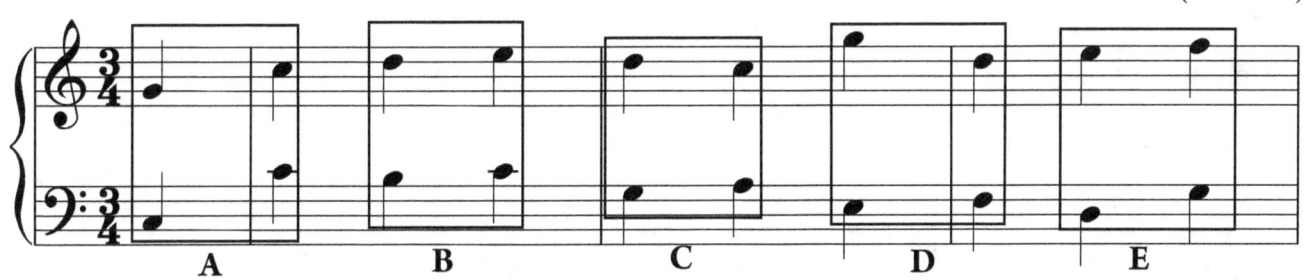

a. Add the correct time signature directly on the music. **3/4**

b. Name the key of this piece. **C major**

c. Name the composer of this piece. **George Frideric Handel**

d. Name another composition by this composer. **Messiah**

d. In what musical era was this composed? **Baroque**

e. This piece is: ☐ monophonic ☑ polyphonic

f. Identify the motion at:

A:	☐ contrary	☐ parallel	☑ similar	☐ oblique
B:	☐ contrary	☑ parallel	☐ similar	☐ oblique
C:	☑ contrary	☐ parallel	☐ similar	☐ oblique
D:	☑ contrary	☐ parallel	☐ similar	☐ oblique
E:	☐ contrary	☐ parallel	☑ similar	☐ oblique
F:	☐ contrary	☐ parallel	☐ similar	☑ oblique

Page 208, No. 1 **Exam Level 7**

G♭ chromatic
D♭ whole tone
C♯ octatonic
E blues
F melodic minor

Page 208, No. 2

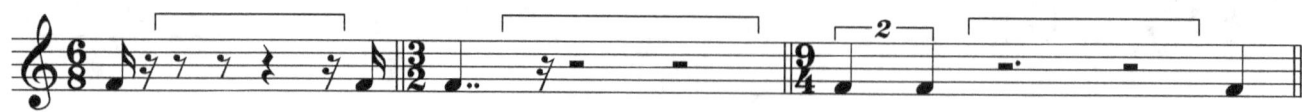

Page 209, No. 3

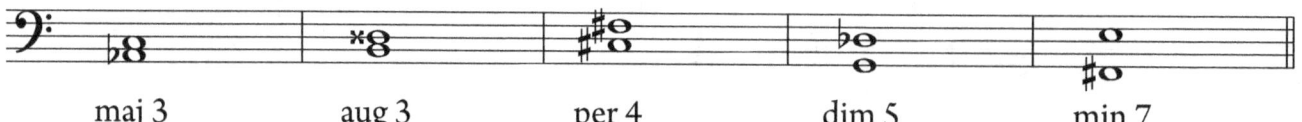

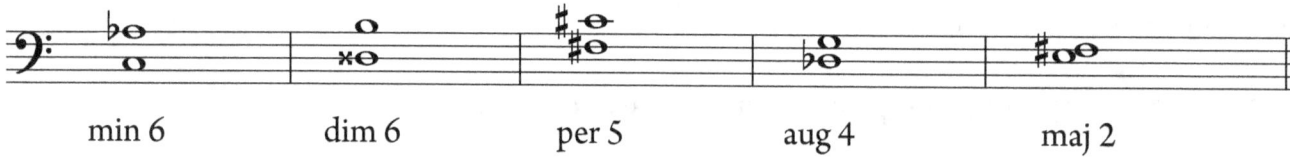

Page 209, No. 4

Page 209, No. 5

original key: G major

Johannes Brahms
Sextet op. 36

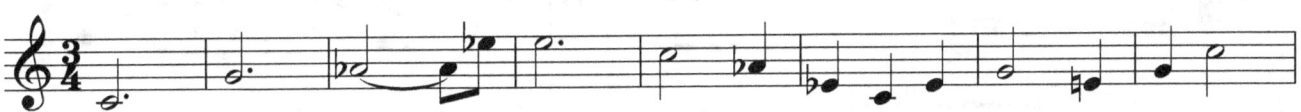

C major

Page 210, No. 6

Page 210, No. 7

d, c, a, e, b

Page 210, No. 8

D minor:	V i	B♭ major:	I V
	perfect authentic		half
C minor:	V i	E major:	IV V
	imperfect authentic		half

Page 211, No. 9

a) C major
b) 2/4
c) C   major   root pos.
d) G   dominant 7th   1st inv.
e) C   major   root pos.
f) G   dominant 7th   root pos.
g) E: passing tones   F: neighbor tone
h) min 2
i) anacrusis or pick up
j) humorous, joyful
k) perfect authentic

Page 211, No. 10

Hugh Le Caine	Modern
Frédéric Chopin	Romantic
Duke Ellington	Modern
Felix Mendelssohn	Romantic
Igor Stravinsky	Modern

Page 212, No. 1 **Exam Level 8**

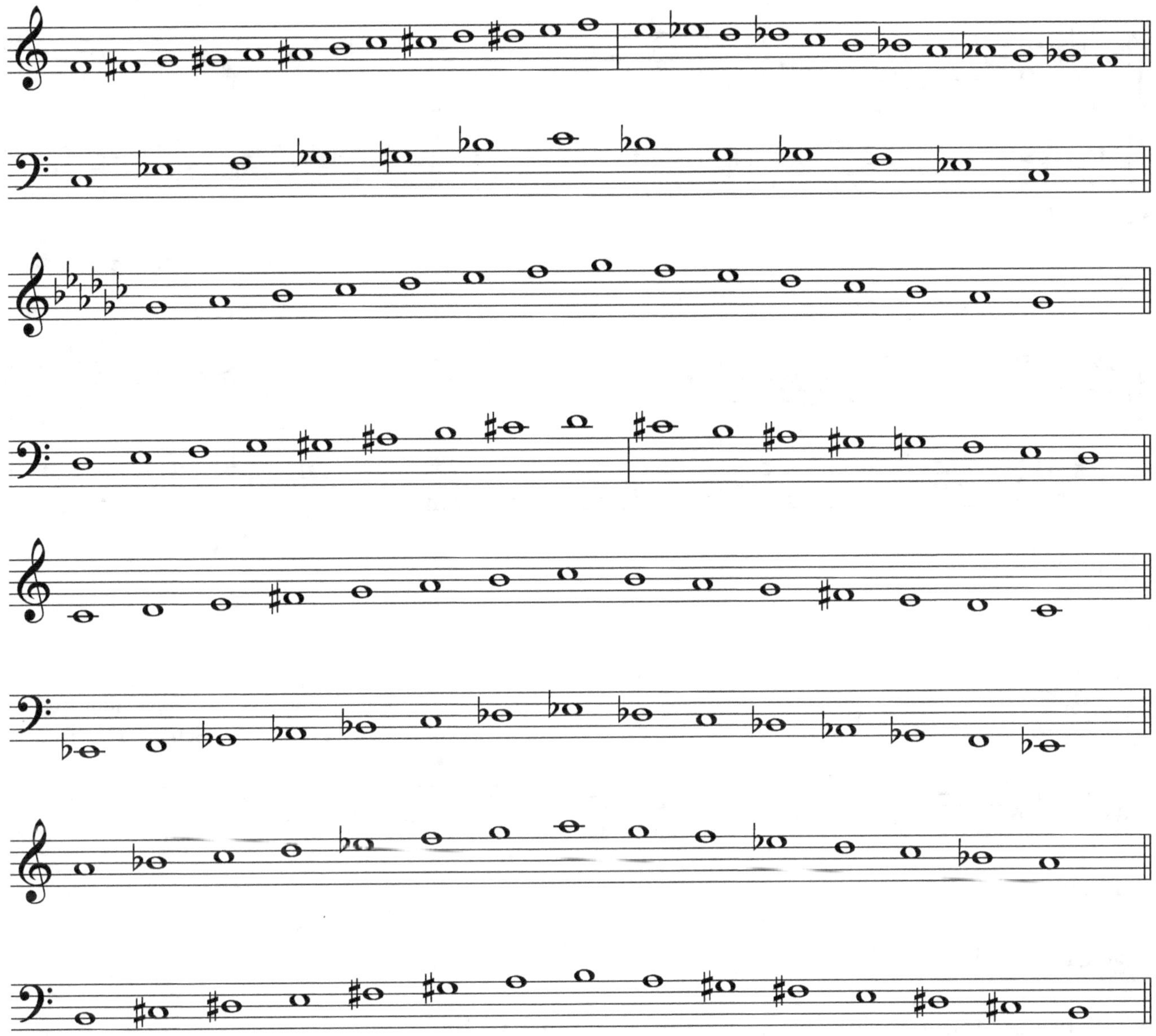

Page 213, No. 2

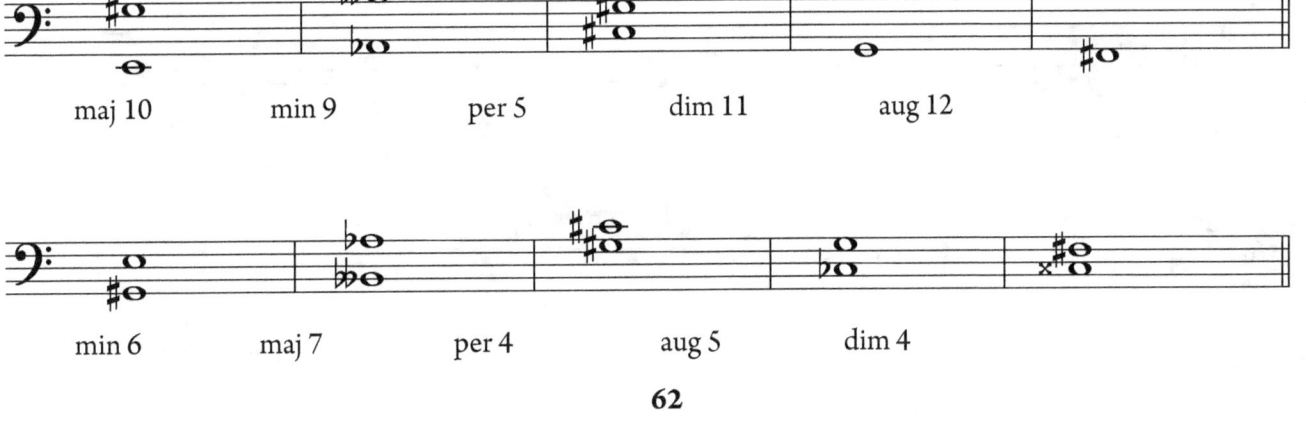

maj 10   min 9   per 5   dim 11   aug 12

min 6   maj 7   per 4   aug 5   dim 4

Page 213, No. 3

Page 213, No. 4

Antonin Dvorak
Scherzo Capriccioso

Page 214, No. 5

minor triad   dominant 7th   quartal chord   diminished 7th
polychord   tone cluster   major triad   diminished triad

Page 214, No. 6

Page 215, No. 7

Page 215, No. 8

Giovanni Croce
Is it Nothing to You?

Page 216, No. 9

a. ritenuto
b. gamelon
c. con sordino
d. raga
e. Josquin des Prez
f. schnell
g. monophony
h. homorhythmic
i. leger
j. Renaissance
k. Hildegard von Bingen
l. polyphony
m. sitar
n. frottola
o. langsam
p. a capella
q. ostinato
r. Medieval
s. tala
t. plainchant

Page 217, No. 10

Ludwig van Beethoven
String Quartet No.16

a) Name the key of this piece. **D flat major**

b) Name the enharmonic tonic minor for this key. **C sharp minor**

c) Write the time signature directly on the score. **6/8**

d) Check two words that describe this time signature:

      ☐simple   ☑**duple**   ☑**compound**   ☐triple   ☐quadruple

e) Name the intervals at A: **maj 3** B: **per 4** C: **per 4**

f) Define **Lento assai: very slow**

g) How are mm. 7, 8, and 9 related? **They are part of a melodic sequence**

h) This is an excerpt from a string quartet. What instument is it written for? **violin**

i) Name the four instruments of the string quartet.

      Violin I Violin II Viola Cello

www.ingramcontent.com/pod-product-compliance
Lightning Source LLC
Chambersburg PA
CBHW080023130526
44591CB00036B/2582